Ethical Business

Restoring Philosophical Integrity

Written by Aubrey Perin

First Edition

Printed in the United States of America

Publisher: pl0rp Media

ISBN: 979-8-9988227-0-4

Cover design by the author

Interior layout by the author

This is a work of nonfiction. All opinions expressed are solely those of the author.

Any references to specific companies or individuals are based on public information and do not constitute endorsement, criticism, or legal accusation.

For information, permissions, or media inquiries, contact: Aubrey.i.perin@gmail.com

Introduction: The Return to Roots

This book was never part of the plan. It was a happy accident — a byproduct of pursuing my MBA while asking one too many philosophical questions in class. What began as a theoretical model to make sense of the national debt evolved into a framework for testing economic integrity itself. And from that spark, a bigger idea emerged: perhaps the market isn't broken in random or chaotic ways. Perhaps it's broken *precisely because* we stopped asking the right questions.

That first model, the Corporate Welfare Equation, did something I didn't expect. It let me take a gut-level reaction ("something's wrong here") and turn it into a testable, falsifiable metric. From there, everything accelerated. I found myself developing frameworks not just for fiscal distortion, but for marketing narratives, accounting practices, and valuation itself. Each one was rooted in logic, refined by philosophical method, and built to be applied — not just debated.

But this isn't a story about finance. It's a story about philosophy in exile.

We've allowed narrative to replace inquiry. "Truth" now arrives prepackaged, algorithmically boosted, and optimized for belief — not for accuracy. In that world, speculation can become value. Hype becomes strategy. Corporations market dreams while selling debt. And we, as a society, pretend this is normal.

The deeper you go into philosophy, the more clearly you see it: the systems we trust were not built on timeless truth. They were built on habit, legacy, and convenience.

1

They grew without rigorous reevaluation. The stories that drive the market are not natural laws — they're unexamined assumptions, repeated until they feel inevitable.

This book is about changing that.

What This Book Is (and Isn't)

This is not a book of rules. It's a book of tests.
It does not preach political doctrine or corporate responsibility slogans. It offers logic-based frameworks that expose distortion and make space for new, better systems to emerge — across industries, ideologies, and institutions.

It is for the intellectually curious. For people who have felt that something is off in the way we assign value, reward innovation, or regulate power — and want tools to make sense of it.

It is not for the comfortable. It is not interested in soothing the disillusioned or mocking the complicit. It does not aim to rescue the system, but to re-root it in reason.

Because all systems — capitalism, accounting, marketing, law — are downstream from philosophical practice. And when we lose the root, we lose the truth.

What Comes Next

In the chapters ahead, you'll find four core frameworks:

- The **Corporate Welfare Equation**: a lens for examining public burden vs. private reward.

- The **ALE Standard**: a restructuring of accounting logic to demand equity, logic, and accountability.

- The **Marketing Integrity Test**: a means to evaluate hype, manipulation, and false scarcity.

- The **Market Integrity Equation**: a method to test whether valuation reflects real-world contribution.

Each of these is rooted in a core belief: that reason is neutral — and *that's* what makes it essential. It isn't reactive. It isn't emotional. It doesn't play favorites. Reason offers us the only tool that can cut through ideology, narrative, and noise to reveal what holds, what breaks, and what must be rebuilt.

We've spent too long arguing from the branches. It's time to go back to the roots.

1   What Business Forgot

Somewhere along the way, business lost the plot.

Once, the idea of business was tied to value — real value. Not the speculative kind, not the perception-driven mirage of momentum investing or brand hype. But value as contribution: the act of creating, exchanging, or delivering something measurable, useful, or necessary. It was tied to things we could see — products built, services delivered, people employed, communities supported.

Trust was once a business asset — not a metric on a dashboard, but a lived relationship. Business was embedded in local ecosystems, accountable to customers and workers alike. Consistent delivery was not just good practice; it was a sign of integrity. Markets functioned as marketplaces — reciprocal, imperfect, but anchored to reality.

But today, the fundamentals that held that world together have been dismantled and replaced. We now live in an age where hype overtakes honesty, where appearance trumps substance, and where visibility alone can be monetized, regardless of whether anything of worth is being created.

The perception of value has become more valuable than value itself. We reward scale before we understand sustainability. We praise disruption before we measure consequences. And increasingly, we see businesses celebrated for growth, not for what they grow.

This Book Is a Response

The distortion we see today is not the result of one bad policy, one irresponsible CEO, or one generation of excess. It is the culmination of a deeper philosophical drift — a slow forgetting of what business is supposed to be, and what principles were once meant to guide it. The idea that value should be created, not just imagined. That systems should be accountable, not just operational. That ethics should be embedded in decision-making, not retrofitted after the damage is done.

We live in a time when unease is ever-present but difficult to articulate. It shows up in moments that feel small but cut deep: a press release full of buzzwords that say nothing. A record-setting bonus issued to a failing executive. A policy initiative wrapped in language about empowerment, while serving only the already empowered. These are not isolated irritants. They are evidence. They are the surface-level symptoms of a system that has traded coherence for performance, and principles for narrative.

This is not about nostalgia. It's not a desire to go backward, nor is it a rejection of progress. The issue is not that business has evolved, but that it has evolved without reflection. Its systems have grown more complex, but less grounded. Its leaders more performative, but less accountable. It has become increasingly difficult to separate what is real from what is constructed. We have arrived at a point where the architecture of value itself is no longer trusted, and where trust, once eroded, cannot be rebuilt through press statements or quarterly targets.

But the sense that something is wrong — that feeling so many carry — is not cynicism. It is clarity in the absence of language. It is an intuition that the metrics being celebrated are not the ones that matter. It is the mind attempting to reconcile a system that no longer mirrors what it claims to represent. And it is a call to reclaim the ability to test that system, not emotionally or ideologically, but logically.

When value is no longer defined by contribution, when ethics become decoration rather than foundation, when business rewards spectacle over substance — what we're left with is not an economy. It's a simulation. And within that simulation, success becomes indistinguishable from spectacle, and failure hides in plain sight, dressed as growth.

The time has come to pierce that illusion. Not with outrage. Not with ideology. But with structure. With logic. With tools that reintroduce clarity to systems that have become opaque by design.

Narrative as the New Ledger

The most potent force in the modern business world isn't capital or labor — it's narrative. Not the kind built through history or lived practice, but the curated, accelerated, and intentionally vague kind, shaped by algorithms and consultants, optimized not for truth but for traction. Narrative has become the new ledger. It defines what is seen, what is rewarded, and ultimately what is remembered.

A business can now exist almost entirely on the strength of its story. Not its product. Not its results. Not its measurable impact. Just the story. A compelling enough narrative can attract capital, earn media praise, avoid scrutiny, and even dictate policy outcomes. Companies that deliver little can raise billions. Those that exploit much can rebrand with a single campaign. Reality becomes an optional feature, not a requirement.

This is not merely distortion — it is inversion. We've inverted the relationship between value and visibility. Instead of value generating visibility, visibility now *confers* value. A firm doesn't need to be viable if it can appear inevitable. And in a landscape dominated by social proof and synthetic metrics, appearance is often all that matters.

What we are witnessing is not innovation — it is theater. Financial theater, performed on spreadsheets and newsfeeds, backed not by contribution but by confidence. And confidence is easy to fabricate when audiences are conditioned to trust momentum over substance.

The tools of this theater are subtle. Buzzwords replace benchmarks. Influence is mistaken for impact. Scarcity is engineered. Urgency is synthetic. And once enough people believe, markets respond — not to what *is*, but to what is *believed to be*. This belief becomes self-fulfilling, until the illusion is mistaken for the truth and the truth becomes irrelevant.

But no performance lasts forever. Systems that run on projection instead of production eventually exhaust their runway. The illusion, no matter how beautifully crafted, cannot conceal the absence of contribution forever. And when that moment comes — when the gap between belief and reality can no longer be maintained — trust collapses. Not just in the performer, but in the stage itself.

What fails in these moments is not just the firm. It's the framework. The deeper damage is done to the legitimacy of business as a system, and to the public's willingness to engage with it in good faith. This is how we reach cynicism. Not because people expect perfection, but because they've been shown — repeatedly — that the performance was never about them.

The fallout is subtle but profound. We begin to question everything, but test nothing. We become suspicious of all success, but unable to distinguish the earned from the engineered. In this state, truth has no anchor and trust has no direction. All that remains is noise.

The Collapse of Inquiry

Once the architecture of value is unmoored from reality, it becomes impossible to sustain coherent systems without deception — intentional or not. What follows is not just economic fragility, but epistemic collapse: a breakdown in how we know what we know. And the first casualty in that collapse is inquiry itself.

Inquiry, at its best, is uncomfortable. It demands friction. It requires that we ask not just "what works," but "why," "for whom," and "at what cost." But modern business, driven by scale and speed, no longer rewards questions with depth. It rewards answers with certainty — preferably short, confident, and backed by data points that support a preexisting story.

What we call "data-driven" today is often just confirmation laundering. The numbers may be accurate, but the questions behind them are shallow. The dashboards are elegant, but the assumptions beneath them go untested. Metrics substitute for meaning. And in this environment, reason itself becomes decorative — something to gesture toward, not to rely on.

Yet ethics, logic, and critical thinking are not afterthoughts to business — they are its foundation.

Without them, incentives mutate. Narratives override math. Accountability becomes optional. And the systems that emerge from this distortion are not just unstable — they are inherently extractive.

We are told we live in an evidence-based world. That performance is tracked, that outcomes are quantifiable, and that data will save us. But in practice, we inhabit a market culture that rewards belief over reality. Anticipation is more profitable than delivery. Promises are monetized long before they are fulfilled — if they are ever fulfilled at all.

This isn't simply economic behavior. It is a philosophical inversion. We have restructured reward mechanisms around speculation, and we are surprised when speculation dominates every layer of the system. The market no longer asks, "What have you done?" It asks, "How much belief can you generate — and how fast?"

In such a system, value is decoupled from contribution. And once that decoupling becomes normalized, belief itself becomes a form of currency — one far easier to manufacture than reality. The result is a marketplace that resembles mythology more than economics. Where the symbols of success are preserved, long after the substance is gone.

This is not sustainable. Not because markets will crash — though they may — but because trust cannot survive prolonged contradiction. When a system claims to reward merit but visibly rewards manipulation, when it speaks of value but trades in perception, the dissonance becomes corrosive. And when belief collapses, there is no ledger left to reconcile.

The only way forward is to return to first principles. Not as a moral preference, but as a survival imperative. We must once again test what we trust. Not with outrage. Not with opinion. But with logic. With reason. With structure.

2   Marketing as Manipulation

Marketing was once a means of communication. It was the interface between a company and the world — an invitation to understand a product, a mission, or a solution. But in the modern economy, marketing has become something else entirely: a tool of behavioral engineering, optimized not to inform, but to provoke. Not to explain, but to extract.

This shift didn't happen all at once. Like the slow replacement of real value with perceived value, marketing's descent into manipulation crept in quietly, hidden behind phrases like "consumer engagement" and "brand storytelling." But beneath the jargon lies a fundamental change in purpose. Where marketing once sought to translate utility into language, it now seeks to generate urgency without context, desire without grounding, and belief without verification.

At its most sophisticated, marketing today functions like a soft form of psychological warfare. It hijacks scarcity instincts. It mimics social cues. It leverages insecurity and FOMO to drive behavior that benefits the brand, not the buyer. And because it's wrapped in the language of innovation, it's rarely questioned — only scaled.

What makes this more dangerous than simple puffery or exaggerated claims is that marketing has moved upstream. It no longer follows the development of a product; it often precedes it. The story is built before the offering exists. The hype is constructed before the functionality is confirmed. The result is a distortion field where narrative drives funding, policy, and public trust before reality is ever tested.

We now live in a world where the promise of a product is more valuable than the product itself — where a startup with a good pitch deck can attract more capital than a functioning small business, and where the signal of innovation carries more weight than actual impact. This is not a side effect of marketing. It is its new design.

Marketing no longer reflects value. It creates the illusion of value, and in doing so, becomes a currency of its own. One that is unregulated, unaccountable, and increasingly untethered from anything testable. This is not just a branding issue. It is a structural one.

And like any unregulated currency, it eventually destabilizes the systems that rely on it.

The logic of modern marketing has inverted the traditional relationship between *concept* and *proof*. Where rigor once demanded evidence before belief, today belief often arrives pre-packaged — crafted with elegance, launched with confidence, and consumed without scrutiny. This is the Figma Fallacy in its purest form: the idea that a well-designed simulation of a product is enough to stand in for the product itself.

In classical reasoning, this would be dismissed as a fallacy of appearance — a confusion between *form* and *function*, between *potential* and *actual*. But in the current economy, this fallacy is rewarded. Tools like Figma — brilliant in their original intent as design mockup platforms — have become emblematic of a deeper philosophical problem: the replacement of verification with presentation.

We no longer ask, *"Does it work?"*
We ask, *"Does it look like it might?"*

The fallacy begins innocently enough: a design team builds a prototype. That prototype is interactive, visually polished, and indistinguishable from a finished product to the untrained eye. Investors are impressed. Screenshots circulate. Hype builds. Before a single line of functional code exists, the company is now perceived as real — not because of what it does, but because of how convincingly it appears to do something.

This is not just bad business practice. It's a breakdown in epistemology. The Figma Fallacy is a symptom of a system where simulation is rewarded more consistently than realization, where aesthetics are treated as evidence, and where narrative *precedes* function in both funding and cultural legitimacy.

It represents a departure from philosophical traditions that privilege substance over style. It trades the slow, deliberate work of validation for the speed and scalability of belief. And the more convincing the simulation, the less the real product is required to exist at all. After all, once the story has gone viral, the substance is a liability — it introduces friction, risk, cost, and accountability.

In this sense, modern marketing doesn't just distort information. It erodes the relationship between appearance and truth. The Figma Fallacy thrives in this erosion, enabling entire companies to raise capital, dominate headlines, and sway markets while offering nothing more than interactive vapor.

And if reality eventually fails to live up to the illusion? That too can be branded. "Beta." "Iterative." "Disruptive pivot." The lexicon of marketing ensures that even failure can be reframed as forward momentum. Because when truth is deferred long enough, trust begins to reset itself around the only thing it has left: the story.

The Figma Fallacy is only one expression of a broader trend — the privileging of perception over substance. But its logic appears everywhere once you know how to see it. Nowhere is that more apparent than in the rise of influencer validation as a surrogate for truth.

Influencers have become the arbiters of legitimacy in domains that once required credentials, experience, or proof. A product endorsed by someone with enough followers is presumed effective. A financial strategy promoted by a charismatic voice on TikTok is presumed sound. A new app or brand, once featured on the right podcast or aesthetic Instagram feed, gains the aura of inevitability — *before a single line of review is written, before a single user tests it in the wild.*

This isn't about malice. It's about infrastructure. The algorithms that determine what we see are optimized for engagement, not integrity. And so we find ourselves in a world where virality and value are increasingly conflated — where the number of views becomes a proxy for the number of verified outcomes.

We mistake reach for proof.

This is not a new mistake, but it is a newly systematized one. The entire apparatus of marketing has learned to borrow the language of community, the rhythms of intimacy, and the cues of trust to bypass the critical scrutiny that would normally attend such claims. When a friend recommends something, we listen. When an influencer simulates that same tone, we internalize the message the same way — but without reciprocity, and without accountability.

In this space, authenticity is manufactured. Behind the curated moments and algorithmically-optimized vulnerability lies a commercial contract. But the consumer doesn't experience it that way. What they experience is *realness*, a sense that the person on the screen actually uses the product, believes in it, has vetted it. They may not even consciously believe it — but the effect is there nonetheless.

This is not just an issue of misplaced trust. It's an issue of distorted epistemology. We are increasingly outsourcing belief formation to those whose incentives are tied not to truth, but to performance. Their ability to shape our perception of a product, a company, or even an economic theory is not tied to accuracy — but to reach, charisma, and alignment with trends that move faster than scrutiny can keep up.

In a world where marketing leads value, the influencer becomes not a guide, but a gatekeeper. Not because they hold deep knowledge — but because they hold attention. And attention, in this system, has been mistaken for authority.

What these examples reveal is not just manipulation — but a quiet, pervasive reordering of how we decide what is real.

The prototype that doesn't function but looks polished, the influencer who appears authentic while performing a contract — these are not anomalies. They are signals of a broader failure: the collapse of epistemic rigor in favor of narrative authority. The rules of proof that once guided evaluation — demonstration, peer review, accountability — have been displaced by signals that merely *feel* like truth: design, popularity, confidence, and repetition.

Marketing, in this context, is no longer about communicating value. It is about replacing the process of discovering truth with the experience of already having found it. It offers comfort before verification, certainty without inquiry, and belonging without context. It bypasses our cognitive defenses by mimicking social trust, exploiting tempo, and overwhelming reflection with exposure.

This would be dangerous in any system. But in business — where perception drives funding, regulation lags behind language, and the consequences of failure are distributed to the public — the risk is not just distortion. It is erosion. Over time, systems that cannot distinguish between belief and fact, between marketing and merit, become brittle. They may grow. They may scale. But they cannot withstand contradiction.

And when the illusion inevitably fractures, the damage is not just to the company that overpromised. It's to the frameworks we use to navigate the world — our sense of what can be trusted, who can be believed, and how decisions should be made. The danger of marketing manipulation is not merely that we buy something that doesn't work. It's that we begin to question whether anything ever did.

That is the deeper harm. Not the scam, but the self-doubt it breeds in its aftermath. And when doubt is widespread, but unaccompanied by tools to test, verify, and rebuild, a vacuum forms. Into that vacuum rushes cynicism, tribalism, and performance — everything but structure.

To resist that spiral, we must not retreat into nostalgia or ideological purity. We must reassert that inquiry matters. That belief should be earned, not manufactured. That appearances must be tested against outcomes. And that marketing, however artful, is not a substitute for integrity — it is a system that must once again be held accountable to it.

Only then can business reclaim its grounding — not through sentiment, but through logic.

3   The Broken Ledger

Every system of trust has its record-keeper.

In business, that role belongs to accounting — a discipline meant to reflect reality in numerical form. The ledger, in theory, is sacred. It is where action becomes evidence, where claims are reconciled with costs, and where equity, liability, and value are made legible. It is supposed to be the mirror of operations, not the mask.

But modern accounting is no longer a reflection of what is. It is a negotiation of what can be justified, deferred, reframed, or obscured. The ledger has become a canvas for financial performance — designed as much for perception as for precision. And as financial instruments grow in complexity, as reporting systems multiply in opacity, what was once a tool of accountability now often functions as a shield from it.

We've come to accept this quietly, even as it erodes the integrity of the systems we depend on. We are told accounting is "just how business works." That GAAP and IFRS are neutral frameworks. That off-balance-sheet obligations, goodwill impairments, or non-GAAP earnings are normal artifacts of a mature market.

But complexity is not the problem. The problem is that these frameworks are no longer bound to first principles. They do not reflect logic. They do not reflect equity. They reflect precedent, preference, and politics. And over time, this has turned one of the most important disciplines in business into a series of permissible distortions, rather than a method of truth-seeking.

The result is what we now live with: a system in which profit can be declared without value created, in which liabilities can be hidden without consequence, and in which long-term obligations are routinely offloaded to the public while short-term gains are privatized and protected.

This is not just a technical issue. It's a philosophical failure. Because when the numbers themselves lose meaning, everything built on top of them becomes suspect.

The language of accounting is often mistaken for clarity. Numbers imply objectivity. Balance sheets imply neutrality. Terms like "assets," "liabilities," and "equity" carry the weight of precision. But language is only as honest as the framework behind it — and in modern accounting, that framework has been hollowed out and replaced with one that prioritizes presentation over meaning.

A liability is no longer simply a debt. It might be an off-balance-sheet agreement, a deferred tax obligation, or a contingent exposure buried in footnotes few will read. Assets may include goodwill inflated by acquisition premiums or brand valuations built on speculative multipliers. And equity, meant to signal residual ownership; can be diluted, deferred, or constructed in ways that leave stakeholders guessing who owns what, and why.

Even the term "earnings" has fractured into multiple definitions: GAAP earnings, adjusted earnings, EBITDA, non-GAAP pro forma results. Each version is technically valid within its own frame — but none are designed to clarify. They are designed to *manage perception*, to highlight the best case and defer the rest. What was once a tool of accountability has become a tool of narrative control, executed through spreadsheets and shareholder letters.

This is not linguistic drift — it is strategic obfuscation. A well-crafted earnings report now resembles a form of marketing: a polished narrative that walks the line between legality and illusion. Complexity becomes camouflage. Ambiguity becomes leverage. And regulators, overwhelmed by volume and precedent, rarely intervene unless deception is catastrophic.

This manipulation of language has consequences. It allows companies to appear stable when they are fragile, profitable when they are not, and ethical while they externalize harm. It confuses shareholders, disempowers employees, and misleads the public into believing that what is reported is what is real.

But the most insidious effect is internal. Over time, businesses begin to believe their own framing. Strategic misrepresentation becomes operational doctrine. Risks are not seen, because they are not reported. Failures are not addressed, because they are offloaded. And in this way, the ledger ceases to be a mirror — and becomes a myth.

A myth of solvency.
A myth of fairness.
A myth of logic in a system designed to evade it.

These distortions aren't just technical inconsistencies. They create structural asymmetries that shape how risk, debt, and responsibility are distributed across society. And more often than not, the distribution is deliberate.

Modern corporations have mastered the art of privatizing gains while socializing losses. The language of accounting makes this possible by rendering certain liabilities invisible — or at least, easily postponed. Pensions are underfunded. Healthcare costs are shifted to workers. Environmental degradation is accounted for as a line-item expense, not a long-term obligation. And when the cumulative weight of these decisions threatens solvency, the response is rarely accountability. It's a bailout.

This dynamic is not incidental. It is woven into the design of our financial systems. A company can extract maximum value through dividends, buybacks, and bonuses during periods of artificial growth — then, when the underlying liabilities surface, it can offload the fallout to governments, insurers, or communities under the justification of systemic risk.

The system rewards this behavior. Executives are rarely held personally accountable for deferred collapses. Investors chase short-term yields without regard for long-term impact. And accounting frameworks, designed to permit flexibility, become instruments of deflection. By the time the bill comes due, the people who profited are gone, and the public is left holding the remainder.

We've seen this cycle across industries. Financial firms in the housing crisis. Energy companies after environmental disasters. Tech companies after market corrections. The patterns repeat, because the incentives remain unchanged — and the accounting structures still enable plausible deniability.

This asymmetry is not just unjust. It is corrosive to the legitimacy of capitalism itself. A market that claims to reward risk must also contain risk. But when risk is hidden, delayed, or externalized, the market ceases to function as a system of feedback — and begins to resemble a shell game, in which the public always ends up paying for the cost of corporate boldness.

Accounting, as it stands, provides the vocabulary for this manipulation. It offers the language to justify imbalance, the categories to obscure responsibility, and the permissions to delay reconciliation until someone else can absorb the impact.

This is the broken ledger:
A system that records *activity*, but not *responsibility*.
That tracks *movement*, but not *meaning*.
That protects perception, even at the cost of reality.

Take the example of goodwill — an intangible asset often created during acquisitions when a company pays more for another business than its net assets are worth on paper. In theory, goodwill represents things like brand value, reputation, or intellectual capital. But in practice, it has become a placeholder for unverified assumptions — a catch-all that allows inflated purchase prices to sit on balance sheets for years without scrutiny.

Goodwill doesn't depreciate like tangible assets. It remains until it is "impaired" — meaning the company has to admit that what it paid for is no longer worth what it once claimed. But impairment is not automatic. It's discretionary. Leadership can postpone recognizing a loss even when it's obvious that the acquired entity isn't delivering on expectations.

This creates a powerful distortion. A company can appear profitable — maintaining a strong balance sheet —

despite having overpaid in ways that will never return value. Meanwhile, that goodwill boosts total asset numbers, making leverage ratios look healthier and giving executives room to justify bonuses, buybacks, and aggressive expansion.

And when impairment finally happens? It often comes too late, after shareholders have bought in, after public trust has been leveraged, and after internal incentives have been extracted.

Goodwill manipulation doesn't always look like fraud. That's what makes it so dangerous. It's not illegal to be optimistic. It's not illegal to be wrong. But when entire industries treat inflated optimism as a strategy — and accounting frameworks allow that optimism to be hidden for years — the system ceases to be a tool of accountability. It becomes a permission structure for institutionalized overreach.

In this way, even a term as seemingly benign as "goodwill" becomes a mechanism of distortion. Not because the word itself is wrong, but because the system allows it to mean whatever is most convenient to the narrative.

The breakdown of accounting is not a failure of numbers — it's a failure of logic.

To restore trust in business systems, we don't just need tighter rules or better enforcement. We need a return to first principles. A framework that doesn't treat accounting as a language of loopholes, but as a structure for truth.

This is the purpose of **ALE** — a standard built on three foundational criteria:

- **Accountable**: Every action, every claim, every entry must have a clear, attributable impact. No externalized harm without notation. No hidden cost without disclosure. Accountability is not a function of timing — it is a function of recognition.

- **Logical**: Financial statements must follow a coherent structure that aligns with real-world causality. Inputs must connect to outputs. Gains must be linked to costs. Accounting cannot be allowed to privilege impression over reasoning. If a transaction doesn't make sense outside of its tax implications, it fails the logic test.

- **Equitable**: Reporting must reflect not just what is legal, but what is fair. Who bears the risk? Who reaps the benefit? ALE demands that accounting disclose asymmetries — not conceal them. If a liability is transferred to the public, the ledger must show it. If a gain is privatized, the ledger must own it.

Together, these three pillars restore accounting as a discipline of truthful reflection, not creative framing.

ALE is not a replacement for GAAP or IFRS. It is a test that sits above them — a philosophical filter designed to expose what traditional accounting allows to remain hidden. Where legacy systems ask, "Does this follow the rules?" ALE asks, "Does this follow reason?"

If a firm's balance sheet passes ALE, its numbers mean something. They represent not just activity, but intent. Not just compliance, but clarity. And that clarity is what has been missing.

In a world where belief is leveraged, perception is monetized, and failure is offloaded, ALE offers something rare: a structure that cannot be manipulated by tone, branding, or timing.

It cannot be spun. It must be earned.

The purpose of ALE is not to punish ambition or constrain innovation. It is to restore coherence. To remind us that business, at its most ethical and sustainable, is not just a set of transactions — it is a system of relationships governed by cause and effect, by trust and truth, by cost and contribution. When accounting forgets that, the systems built on top of it begin to fail. But with a structure like ALE, we remember what accounting is supposed to do: not just keep records, but keep us honest. Because in a world saturated with spectacle, logic may be the last remaining form of integrity.

4   Bipartisan Betrayal

Markets don't break themselves.

For every distortion in business practice, there is a corresponding failure in governance — a loophole left open, a rule selectively enforced, a campaign donation exchanged for silence. The illusion of value that dominates modern markets didn't emerge in a vacuum. It was *enabled* by the very institutions designed to ensure transparency, fairness, and public accountability.

This is the quiet betrayal that defines our era: not corruption in the form of overt scandal, but a subtler, bipartisan complicity — a mutual agreement to look away while the architecture of the economy is reshaped to serve the few.

Both major political parties have participated. Both have claimed the language of responsibility while legislating irresponsibility into permanence. One does it in the name of freedom. The other in the name of stability. But the outcome is the same: regulation designed to fail, oversight bodies left underfunded, tax codes written in pencil by lobbyists and signed in ink by lawmakers who call it compromise.

This is not ideological imbalance. It is *symmetry in abdication.* One party pushes deregulation, calling it pro-growth. The other negotiates guardrails so soft they dissolve on contact. The result is a political culture where accountability is performative, where policy follows capital, and where public interest is redefined in quarterly terms.

Meanwhile, those who speak of reform are cast as naive. Those who ask foundational questions are told to be practical. And those who profit from the status quo remind us — repeatedly — that the system, for all its flaws, is "working."

And they're right.

It is working — as designed.
Just not for you.

To understand how bipartisan failure becomes structural, we must look at the machinery that makes it possible: lobbying.

Lobbying is often discussed in polite terms — as advocacy, as consultation, as the democratic right of industries to inform policymakers. But in its modern form, lobbying is not dialogue. It is design. It is how laws are written *before* debate begins, how language is inserted into bills that no one claims to have authored, how incentives are structured so that accountability is impossible even in hindsight.

Lobbying has become the preferred mode of legislation, not because it's effective in serving the public — but because it works *perfectly* for those with something to protect. It is the hidden draft layer of American lawmaking, where bills are sculpted not in committee chambers, but in conference rooms staffed by former regulators, retired politicians, and legal architects paid to ensure that loopholes are not accidents, but assets.

This is not influence. It is institutionalized preference. And it exists on both sides of the aisle.

In moments of political theater, one party may shout down corporate excess while the other defends it. But behind closed doors, both rely on the same donors, the same think tanks, the same lobbyist briefings that distill complex legislation into two-page talking points and pre-approved soundbites. Whether it's deregulation in energy, subsidies in agriculture, or patent law in technology, the fingerprints of lobbying are everywhere — and the people whose lives are affected by these policies are almost never in the room.

The result is a governance structure that speaks the language of choice while delivering the outcomes of monopoly. And just as monopolies in business distort markets, monopolies of influence distort democracy.

What we are left with is a system in which:

- Regulation is shaped by those it is meant to restrain.

- Public benefit is redefined as market alignment.

- Political accountability is measured not in results, but in donations raised and airtime earned.

This is not conspiracy. It is process. Legal. Public. Documented. And persistent.

And it is why meaningful reform so rarely survives translation into law. Not because lawmakers are powerless — but because many of them are functionaries of a system that rewards the appearance of conflict while delivering consensus behind the curtain.

Consensus that says:

- The market knows best.

- Corporations are people.

- Growth excuses everything.

This is how bipartisan betrayal hides in plain sight — not as gridlock, but as agreement in all the wrong places.

For the average citizen, the political landscape appears fractured — partisan warfare, ideological polarization, cultural division. It's exhausting by design. Each news cycle delivers fresh outrage. Each debate is framed as existential. Each election is sold as the most important in history.

But beneath the noise lies a quiet truth: there is far less disagreement than we are led to believe.

The illusion of opposition is perhaps the most effective political product ever marketed. It keeps citizens engaged but disoriented, inflamed but powerless. It casts politics as a battleground of ideas, while in reality, it is often a marketplace of influence, where the real fights are not about values — but about *who gets to write the rules, and who they serve.*

Both parties speak of justice, but neither addresses the tax code that allows multinational corporations to pay nothing while public schools crumble. Both speak of opportunity, but neither challenges the structures that make upward mobility mathematically improbable for most. Both claim to protect democracy, yet accept funding from the same corporate donors and vote in lockstep on legislation that expands surveillance, privatizes essential services, and shields financial actors from consequence.

This isn't ideological diversity — it's a conflict of aesthetics. Red vs. blue. Urban vs. rural. Progressive vs. conservative. The labels change. The spectacle evolves. But the underlying policies — those that shape wealth concentration, corporate power, regulatory enforcement, and public debt — remain largely untouched.

The script is well-rehearsed:

- One party champions "free enterprise," while quietly ensuring bailouts for the largest players.

- The other champions "the working class," while partnering with consultants who engineer outsourced labor and gig economy loopholes.

- Both point fingers during crisis, but vote together when corporations need relief.

- Neither takes responsibility when inequality deepens or infrastructure fails or a preventable collapse is "suddenly" unavoidable.

This isn't failure. It's performance.

It gives the appearance of choice while narrowing its real consequences. It allows citizens to vent without shifting power. And perhaps most importantly, it makes systemic reform appear impossible — because if both sides are fighting, surely someone must be trying to fix it.

But no one is. Not meaningfully. Not structurally. And the longer we believe that this conflict is real, the longer we remain part of the act.

This is the final betrayal: not just of policy, but of hope. The transformation of civic engagement into brand loyalty, where political identity replaces principle, and belief in better systems is dismissed as naïve.

But clarity is not naïveté. And understanding is not cynicism. To expose the illusion is not to despair — it is to begin again, this time with structure.

The erosion of trust in governance isn't just the result of collusion or cowardice. Sometimes, it's the product of something quieter and harder to see: institutional forgetfulness.

Regulatory agencies, watchdogs, and oversight bodies were not always passive. Many were born out of crisis — The SEC after the Great Depression, the EPA after environmental collapse, labor protections after industrial abuse. They were designed to ensure that memory — of harm, failure, exploitation — was codified into law.

But over time, that memory fades. Regulations are softened, rewritten, or repealed. Agency budgets are cut. Expertise is hollowed out. Institutional knowledge walks out the door and is not replaced. And what began as a mission to protect the public becomes an exercise in maintaining appearances.

This is not because regulators are inherently weak or corrupt. It's because the systems they operate in are not designed to retain clarity without constant reinforcement. And in a culture where lobbying is relentless and narratives are weaponized, reinforcement rarely arrives.

Instead, what takes root is a form of procedural amnesia — a slow forgetting of why certain safeguards existed, of what past abuses looked like, of what collapse costs. And once forgotten, those lessons must be relearned. Usually through crisis.

This is how entire industries reset their boundaries:

- By pushing past them,

- Waiting for failure,

- Then negotiating the consequences on favorable terms.

The failure here is not simply one of political will, but of philosophical grounding. Without a shared commitment to first principles — accountability, logic, equity — even the best laws become brittle, and the best institutions become reactive. They remember just enough to appear credible, but not enough to act with foresight.

And so the cycle continues.
Spectacle replaces structure.
Crisis replaces reform.
And trust, once broken, is left unrebuilt.

But forgetting is not irreversible.
What has been eroded can be restored.
Not with outrage. Not with tribalism.
But with systems designed to remember — and built to withstand forgetting.

5 The Corporate Welfare Equation

For all its complexity, the modern economy runs on a simple story: that profit signals success, that private enterprise drives innovation, and that the role of government is to enable, not interfere. This story has been told so often, and with such confident repetition, that it now feels like a law of nature — something to be managed, not questioned.

But stories can be tested. And when we test this one, we begin to see cracks.

We are told that private enterprise bears risk. Yet in crisis, the state absorbs it. We are told that markets reward efficiency. Yet the most bloated institutions receive the most assistance. We are told that government should stay out of business. Yet entire sectors are sustained by public spending, tax incentives, legal shields, and bailout guarantees.

What we are looking at is not capitalism in its pure form. It is a system of selective intervention — one in which risk is privatized when profitable and socialized when not. This system has a name. It is not "free enterprise." It is corporate welfare.

And for years, it has been allowed to operate without measurement.

That's where the Corporate Welfare Equation (CWE) begins: as a tool to expose this asymmetry. A way to quantify what is normally hidden behind financial abstraction and political rhetoric. A test to determine

whether a company is operating within a fair market —
or floating on the cushion of public subsidy, legal
distortion, or deferred liability.

The equation is simple in form, but potent in implication.
It asks a single question:

What is the net public cost of your private success?

And it answers that question not in sentiment, but in
structure — by tracking government assistance, regulatory
shelter, tax avoidance, and externalized harm against
declared profitability and shareholder return.

When those inputs are tallied, a new kind of balance sheet
emerges. One that tells a different story. One that does
not just celebrate performance, but interrogates
dependency.

Because in a truly free market, success should not require
a hidden scaffold of public risk. And if it does, that
dependency should be visible, measurable, and subject to
accountability.

That is what CWE offers: not a condemnation, but a
calibration — a way to restore clarity where narrative has
taken root.

We don't need hypotheticals to justify this equation. We
live inside its proof.

Take the airline industry. Airlines operate on tight
margins and enormous leverage. When times are good,
they execute stock buybacks and reward shareholders.
When crisis hits — as it did during the COVID-19
pandemic — they are among the first in line for public
assistance. In 2020, U.S. airlines received tens of billions

of dollars in government bailouts, much of it with few strings attached. The justification was economic stability. The result was privatized gain, publicly insured risk — and within a year, layoffs, executive bonuses, and resumed buybacks.

Or consider the fossil fuel industry. For decades, oil and gas companies have received enormous federal subsidies, tax breaks, and preferential treatment in both policy and infrastructure. These benefits are rarely acknowledged in annual reports, yet they shape every part of the industry's pricing model. Meanwhile, the long-term environmental costs — oil spills, water pollution, atmospheric degradation — are absorbed by the public through cleanup efforts, healthcare systems, and climate-related infrastructure strain.

Big Tech offers another example. Companies like Amazon, Google, and Meta build immense valuations through global reach and data monetization — yet they benefit from tax minimization strategies, regulatory inaction, and intellectual property protections that were often developed and subsidized by public research. Their platforms exploit infrastructure they do not pay for — roads, electrical grids, undersea cables, spectrum licenses — and their negative externalities, like disinformation and digital addiction, are offloaded to public institutions, schools, and mental health providers.

Even the pharmaceutical industry, often heralded for innovation, is built on a hidden public foundation. Many of the most profitable drugs originate in federally funded research labs, then are commercialized by private firms that set prices inaccessible to the very taxpayers who helped create them. The risk is socialized. The reward is monopolized.

These are not exceptions. They are the operating model.

And yet, in every earnings call, every political debate, and every economic white paper, these industries are still framed as champions of free enterprise — lean, efficient, self-made.

This is the illusion that the Corporate Welfare Equation is built to expose. Not as a tool for judgment, but as a tool for clarity. Because before we can reform a system, we must be able to see it. And right now, we see only the surface.

The rest has been absorbed — by governments, by communities, by future generations — with no line item to mark its cost.

To understand the logic of the Corporate Welfare Equation, imagine a company that appears wildly successful.

Its revenues are strong. Its stock price is climbing. Its leadership is praised for vision and agility. And on the surface, everything looks like textbook capitalism: a well-run enterprise delivering value and being rewarded for it.

But now ask a different set of questions:

- How much of that "success" is made possible by tax credits or deferred liabilities?

- How much of its infrastructure is built on public investment it didn't pay for?

- How much of its workforce is underpaid, with the difference made up by government programs?

- How many of its risks are backstopped by subsidies, guarantees, or legal shields that no small business could ever access?

- And how much of its environmental, social, or logistical impact is externalized — handled not by the company, but by hospitals, schools, cleanup crews, or future generations?

These questions rarely appear in annual reports. But they represent real costs — just not to the company. To everyone else.

Now apply the equation.

The CWE begins by identifying the invisible inputs — the public scaffolding that holds the firm aloft:

- Government subsidies or bailouts

- Regulatory shelters or non-enforcement

- Unpaid externalities (e.g. pollution, algorithmic harm, labor underpayment)

- Use of public infrastructure or research without reciprocal investment

- Tax avoidance strategies that shift burden to others

It then sets those costs against declared success metrics:

- Revenue and profit margins

- Executive compensation

- Dividends and stock buybacks

- Market capitalization

What emerges is a clearer picture of *who is actually carrying the weight.*

A company that reports $3 billion in annual profit but receives $1.5 billion in direct and indirect public benefit is not producing $3 billion in value. It is offloading half its costs — and capturing the difference as reward.

This doesn't mean the company is evil. It means the system has no internal correction. CWE simply reintroduces a logic test. It asks:

Is this profit self-generated — or borrowed from public risk and unrecognized labor?

It reframes financial success not as a celebration, but as a question. And in doing so, it exposes the true character of the economy we've built — one in which dependency is hidden beneath the surface, and perception is managed through selective omission.

The CWE is not a judgment. It's a mirror.

And for many institutions, it will be the first time they've seen themselves in full.

The Corporate Welfare Equation (CWE)

At its core, the Corporate Welfare Equation asks a simple question:

How much of a company's success is derived from publicly funded, publicly absorbed, or publicly ignored costs?

It does this by contrasting public dependency with declared profitability. The equation is designed to isolate and expose the extent to which a company's earnings are buoyed by unaccounted public contributions — fiscal, legal, social, or environmental.

Here is the basic form:

$$\mathbf{CWE} = \frac{\text{Declared Profit}}{\text{Declared Profit} + \text{Public Contribution}}$$

Where:

- **Declared Profit** includes net income, retained earnings, stock buybacks, and executive compensation — any monetary metric used to claim corporate success.

- **Public Contribution** includes:

    o **Subsidies** (direct or indirect)

    o **Bailouts or financial guarantees**

    o **Tax avoidance** (effective rate vs. statutory)

    o **Externalized costs** (e.g., environmental degradation, underpaid labor offset by public assistance)

    o **Use of public infrastructure or R&D without proportionate investment**

    o **Regulatory privileges or deregulatory carve-outs**

The resulting CWE score ranges from 0 to 1:

- A CWE of 1.0 suggests the company operates with no measurable public support — success is internally derived.

- A CWE of 0.5 indicates that for every dollar of profit, another dollar of hidden public cost exists.

- A CWE below 0.5 signals severe dependency — a firm whose perceived success is built more on public accommodation than private contribution.

Why It Matters

Most modern firms do not report these figures side-by-side. Earnings are declared with precision; public benefit is implied or omitted. Tax breaks are celebrated in investor calls, but not disclosed in financial statements. Regulatory favors are treated as market conditions. And externalities — unless forced into the open — remain invisible.

The CWE exposes these blind spots by restructuring the narrative. It doesn't change the numbers. It changes what they mean.

Because profit without accountability is not success. It's subsidized storytelling.

Example: Company A

Company A is a household name — praised for innovation, profitability, and rapid growth. In its latest annual report, it declares:

- **$1.2 billion** in net income

- **$400 million** in stock buybacks

- **$100 million** in executive compensation

- **$0 corporate income tax paid**, due to overseas tax shelters and carried losses

Total **Declared Profit** = $1.7 billion

But here's what doesn't appear in the shareholder letter:

- **$600 million** in government subsidies and tax credits (green energy incentives, relocation tax holidays, local infrastructure grants)

- **$400 million** in labor externalities, as thousands of employees qualify for federal food assistance and Medicaid due to suppressed wages

- **$300 million** in deferred environmental cleanup costs stemming from industrial byproducts, with no escrow set aside

- **$150 million** in unpaid infrastructure usage — public roads, energy grids, subsidized internet access — factored into operational savings

- **$50 million** in unregulated data extraction and content moderation costs pushed onto schools, nonprofits, and government agencies

Total **Public Contribution** = $1.5 billion

Now apply the Corporate Welfare Equation:

$$\mathbf{CWE = \frac{1.7}{1.7 + 1.5} = \frac{1.7}{3.2} \approx 0.53}$$

This tells us something simple but powerful: nearly half of Company A's apparent success is built on public support — support not reflected in its valuation, not reimbursed through taxation, and not acknowledged in public discourse.

A traditional balance sheet would call this company efficient.
The market would call it a winner.
CWE calls it what it is: **dependent**.

Not unprofitable. Not villainous.
But deeply enmeshed in a system of support it does not disclose.

That's the insight CWE provides. Not to vilify, but to measure. To place side-by-side what companies claim — and what the public carries. To bring the hidden economy of corporate reliance into full view.

How to Interpret a CWE Score

The Corporate Welfare Equation is not a moral verdict — it's a visibility tool.

A high CWE score (closer to 1.0) indicates that a company's profits are primarily self-derived, with minimal measurable reliance on public scaffolding. This suggests operational independence and internal accountability — what traditional capitalism claims to reward.

A mid-range CWE score (around 0.5) indicates a business model that is equally reliant on public input and private effort. This doesn't make it unethical — but it calls into question whether the firm should be celebrated as a paragon of efficiency or innovation. It suggests that the public is co-producing the profit, often without shared benefit.

A low CWE score (below 0.5) indicates significant dependence on hidden support. The company's success is propped up by external structures, many of which are paid for or maintained by taxpayers, regulators, or vulnerable labor. In these cases, the company's valuation may be overstated — not because the market is irrational, but because the *accounting of inputs* is incomplete.

CWE is not designed to shame businesses. It is designed to recalibrate expectations.

In a world where private success is often framed as evidence of moral virtue, CWE reminds us that context matters. Profit divorced from responsibility is not proof of excellence — it is proof of permission. And until we understand the scaffolding beneath profitability, we cannot design systems that are truly fair, sustainable, or self-correcting.

The CWE does not tell us who to trust.
It tells us who to test.
And what questions to finally start asking.

What CWE Unveils

Every time a company externalizes a cost — through a bailout, a subsidy, a deferred cleanup, or a tax avoidance scheme — that cost doesn't disappear. It simply moves.

And in most cases, it moves to the same place: the national debt.

That debt is not an abstract economic artifact. It is a delayed invoice for decisions made in favor of short-term corporate stability at the expense of long-term public solvency. It reflects not just wars or infrastructure or stimulus packages, but decades of structural

45

accommodation for firms deemed "too big to fail" or "too valuable to challenge."

When governments absorb corporate risk, underwrite losses, and suppress accountability in the name of economic continuity, they are not solving problems — they are borrowing against them.

And that borrowed cost lands squarely on the public balance sheet.

What we call the national debt is often a backlog of private dependency dressed up in patriotic language. It is the price we pay to maintain the illusion that our largest firms operate independently, that markets self-correct, and that public intervention is the exception rather than the rule.

But the CWE reveals a different truth:

The national debt is the passive ledger of corporate welfare.
It is not a measure of irresponsibility.
It is a measure of political permission — granted without accounting, and inherited without consent.

Once we understand this, debates about austerity, taxation, and spending take on a different character. They are no longer about "living within our means." They are about deciding who pays for whose success — and when.

Why Existing Metrics Fail

Most economic narratives today rely on metrics that appear authoritative but are structurally blind to public dependency.

The price-to-earnings ratio tells us how much investors are willing to pay for a company's earnings — but says nothing about how those earnings were produced, or what portion of the cost was deferred to the public.

Tax revenue data shows what governments collect — but not what should have been collected, nor what was quietly forgiven through loopholes and carveouts.

ESG scores attempt to measure ethical conduct — but often privilege superficial disclosure over structural accountability, allowing companies to rank high while engaging in aggressive offshoring, greenwashing, or labor suppression.

Even national productivity statistics and GDP growth figures bundle externalized harm into positive indicators. When a company avoids taxes or underpays workers, GDP still rises. When the government absorbs corporate loss, GDP doesn't decline — it grows. The system records activity, not fairness. It records profit, not justice. It records scale, not sustainability.

These metrics were not built to tell the full story. They were built to tell a useful story — one that supports belief in market efficiency, reinforces investor confidence, and minimizes the appearance of systemic imbalance.

But belief is not clarity.
And confidence is not truth.

CWE is different because it starts from a first principle that modern metrics omit:

That not all profit is created equally — and not all value is privately earned.

By reintroducing accountability to success, CWE exposes a dimension of business performance that traditional indicators are designed to ignore. It doesn't replace existing tools — it reveals their blind spots.

And once those blind spots are seen, they can't be unseen. The public cost of private gain is no longer a philosophical concern or a political talking point. It becomes a number. And numbers have gravity.

From Exposure to Design

The Corporate Welfare Equation gives us something we've never had: a means to make the invisible visible, to quantify dependency where independence was assumed, and to ask new questions about what success should mean in a society where risk is so often offloaded and reward so narrowly distributed.

But exposure is only the first step.
Clarity without structure leaves us aware — but stranded.
We can now see which companies depend on public scaffolding.
But what does it look like to build differently?

To restore trust in business, we need more than transparency.
We need a new logic of accounting — one that doesn't just record activity, but honors accountability, coherence, and shared cost.

We need a ledger that doesn't just tell a story to investors, but tells the truth to everyone else.

And that's where we begin next.

6   The ALE Standard

For decades, accounting has been treated as neutral ground — a discipline of numbers, rules, and compliance. But numbers alone do not create clarity. Structure does. Logic does. Values do.

What we call "generally accepted accounting principles" were never neutral. They are the result of negotiated assumptions — assumptions that prioritize investor clarity, short-term reporting, and legal minimalism over public accountability or moral coherence. In a system optimized for perception, even the ledger can become a tool of performance.

To restore truth to accounting, we must return it to its philosophical roots.

That is the purpose of the ALE Standard.

ALE stands for:

- Accountable

- Logical

- Equitable

Three criteria. One filter. ALE is not a new set of debits and credits. It is a higher-order test that sits above them — a method to evaluate whether financial statements reflect reality, responsibility, and fairness.

Because every company may follow the rules — but not every company is telling the truth.
And when truth is obscured, so is risk. So is harm. So is trust.

The ALE Standard challenges business not to comply —
but to cohere. It invites companies to ask:

- Does this statement reflect who pays the cost and
  who reaps the benefit?

- Does it follow cause and effect — not just
  convention?

- Would this balance sheet make sense if read by
  someone outside the firm — someone affected by
  its decisions?

When ALE is applied, these are not philosophical
luxuries.
They are operational necessities.
Because in a world where confidence is manufactured and
complexity is exploited, logic becomes the only remaining
safeguard.

The ALE Standard: What It Tests

Each element of ALE captures a different failure mode in
modern accounting. Together, they form a philosophical
filter — simple in form, but powerful in implication. To
pass ALE, a company's financial statements must
demonstrate all three: Accountability, Logic, and Equity.

1. Accountable: Who pays, who decides, and who is left
out?

Accountability begins with recognition.

It demands that every cost, risk, and consequence be
placed in the ledger — not just those that affect investors,
but those that affect workers, communities, and
governments. It requires that businesses record not just

50

the outcome of their choices, but the real distribution of their impact.

This means:

- Externalities must be acknowledged, not ignored.

- Subsidies and tax breaks must be disclosed as structural inputs.

- Labor underpayment must be counted as a public liability — not a margin enhancer.

A business passes the Accountable test if its success can be explained without omitting who absorbed the cost of its growth. If a firm appears profitable only because key liabilities were deferred, hidden, or passed on to the public — it fails.

2. Logical: Does the financial narrative follow cause and effect?

Logic is the foundation of all structure. A ledger must reflect reality — not just regulatory permission.

A business passes the Logical test if its financial statements align with causal reasoning. Revenue must be tied to production, cost must follow activity, and assets must be grounded in provable value — not inflated forecasts or speculative goodwill.

This test catches:

- Accounting games like booking revenue before delivery.

- Treating marketing hype as valuation input.

- Misstating costs through off-balance-sheet vehicles or deferred impairments.

If a financial statement looks good but doesn't make sense, it fails the logic test. Because in any coherent system, success must follow from substance — not from omission or illusion.

3. Equitable: Does this reflect a fair share of cost and gain?

Equity doesn't mean every stakeholder is treated the same — it means they are recognized in proportion to their contribution and exposure.

The Equitable test examines whether a company's reports reflect the real power dynamics and risk distribution of its operations:

- Are workers treated as cost centers while executives absorb all surplus?

- Are public services used without reinvestment?

- Are risk protections privatized while downside is socialized?

A company fails the Equitable test if its accounting treats support structures as invisible, while concentrating profit in a narrow class of beneficiaries. In other words: if the public carries the weight but gets none of the lift.

Why ALE Works

Each test reveals a different kind of distortion:

- Accountable captures omissions.

- Logical captures contradictions.

- Equitable captures imbalance.

Where GAAP asks, *"Did you follow the rules?"*
ALE asks, *"Does this reflect reality, responsibility, and fairness?"*

Together, the ALE Standard transforms accounting from a record of claims into a test of coherence. It brings ethics back to the ledger — not as sentiment, but as structure.

The Ledger Illusion

There is a quiet assumption in modern accounting:

If it's on the books, it must be true.

But like the Figma Fallacy — where a clickable mockup is mistaken for a working product — the Ledger Illusion convinces us that a balance sheet, if formatted properly, reflects reality. It doesn't.

Accounting frameworks today are built to tell stories to investors, not truths to society. Revenue can be recognized before value is delivered. Costs can be moved off-balance-sheet. Risk can be deferred indefinitely. And as long as the formatting complies with GAAP or IFRS, the illusion holds.

This is the Ledger Illusion: the idea that compliance equals coherence, and that the presence of structure implies the presence of substance.

We see it when:

- Goodwill is listed as an asset based on branding, not economic contribution.

- Offloaded pension plans reduce liabilities without disclosing public absorption.

- Deferred maintenance is excluded from cost modeling while share prices climb.

Everything *adds up*.
But it doesn't *make sense*.

Just like the Figma prototype, the ledger functions as a simulation — an elegant narrative that feels functional, but hasn't yet been tested against reality.

ALE is designed to break that illusion.

It asks not just whether the books are clean, but whether they're honest. Whether they follow reason. Whether they account for impact. Whether they represent the world as it is — not just the version that's easiest to present.

Because until we disrupt the Ledger Illusion, business will continue to pass every test — except the ones that matter.

ALE Formula: The Expanded Balance Sheet

The ALE Logic Test doesn't just ask *philosophical* questions — it introduces a structural upgrade. It redefines what a balance sheet should reflect: not just ownership and obligations, but truth, cause, and consequence.

To accomplish this, ALE reformulates the three major financial categories:

Assets (A)

$$A = A_{real} + A_{social} + A_{extracted} + A_{unearned}$$

- **A_real**: Tangible and intangible productive assets — factories, systems, patents.

- **A_social**: Public infrastructure, subsidized education, labor supported by public benefits.

- **A_extracted**: Gains obtained through underpayment, rent-seeking, or legal exploitation.

- **A_unearned**: Speculative gains driven by branding, hype, or market distortion.

This logic forces firms to declare *where value comes from* — not just what it's worth.

Liabilities (L)

$$L = L_{\text{reported}} + L_{\text{externalized}}$$

- **L_reported**: Traditional debts, leases, financial obligations.

- **L_externalized**: Environmental damage, public health impacts, social burdens.

This reorients accountability. If the public absorbs the cost, it still belongs on the balance sheet.

Equity (E)

$$E = E_{\text{contributed}} + E_{\text{inflated}} - E_{\text{extractive}} - E_{\text{recursive}}$$

- **E_contributed**: Actual stakeholder value — retained earnings, reinvestment.

- **E_inflated**: EPS boosts from buybacks and artificial scarcity.

- **E_extractive**: Value gained by suppressing wages or exploiting risk gaps.

- **E_recursive**: Insider equity recycled to control the firm (self-voting risk).

This component exposes how value is distributed — and who controls it.

Depreciation Disparity: Favoring Machines Over People

ALE also spotlights systemic bias in the logic of tax accounting.

Let:

- **DC** = Depreciation of capital (equipment, machines)

- **DL** = Depreciation of labor (workers leaving, retiring, replaced)

- **T_DC** = Tax deduction for capital depreciation

- **T_DL** = Tax deduction for labor loss (currently: none)

Logic violation:

$$DC \Rightarrow T_{DC} \quad \text{and} \quad DL \nRightarrow T_{DL} \Rightarrow \text{Incoherence}$$

If machines losing value reduce tax burdens, but workers losing relevance do not, the logic of economic decay and reinvestment collapses. It privileges capital over people and treats labor as expendable and invisible.

Recursive Ownership: When Firms Become Their Own Biggest Shareholder

In conventional finance, stock buybacks are framed as shareholder value. But ALE surfaces their feedback-loop logic — especially when combined with executive equity awards.

Variables:

- **SB** = Stock Buybacks
- **EO** = Executive Ownership
- **CP** = Corporate Control
- **S_total** = Total shares
- **S_corp + S_exec** = Insider-controlled shares
- **S_max_individual** = Largest external shareholder

Governance Logic Violations:

1. **Self-Voting Risk:**
   If the corporation owns more shares than any single external holder:

$$S_{\text{corp}} \geq S_{\text{max\_individual}} - \varepsilon \Rightarrow \text{Corporate self-ownership}$$

2. **Privatized Control Risk:**
   If insider-controlled shares exceed 50% of the total float:

$$(S_{\text{corp}} + S_{\text{exec}})/S_{\text{total}} \geq 0.5 \Rightarrow \text{Privatized governance}$$

Implication:
Market signaling fails. Power is consolidated. External checks vanish. Accountability collapses.

Why This Matters

This expanded ALE logic isn't just academic — it surfaces truths that legacy accounting frameworks are structurally incapable of capturing. It reveals:

- How earnings are inflated through public subsidy

- How risk is offloaded to the taxpayer while control is consolidated

- How the system continues to reward opacity under the guise of performance

And it offers a path forward — not through punitive reform, but through coherent design.

Because if business is to be ethical, it must also be rational.
And if it cannot pass a logic test —
Then it cannot be trusted to pass any other.

Expanding ALE Through Systemic Correctives

While the ALE Standard reveals how modern accounting fails to reflect fairness, these four constructs operationalize reform. They do not merely diagnose — they propose pressure points for restoring logical and moral integrity to the balance sheet.

1. Depreciation Disparity (DD): Accounting's Bias for Capital Over Labor

Modern accounting allows capital assets to depreciate — machinery, buildings, software — which in turn reduces taxable income. But labor, which also diminishes over time (through burnout, skill atrophy, aging), has no analogous treatment.

This creates a logic violation:

- Machines become cheaper to own the longer you hold them.

- Humans become more expensive — despite also decaying in value under the firm's use.

Implication:
This accounting asymmetry favors automation and underinvestment in people. It treats human contribution as expense, while treating capital as an investment to be optimized.

ALE Intervention:
Expose this imbalance on the balance sheet. If companies claim depreciation on trucks, but fire aging workers to avoid rising healthcare costs, the ledger should show this as an equity violation.

This isn't about inflating labor costs. It's about acknowledging human capital as capital.

2. Recursive Equity (RE): When Corporations Own Their Own Power

Stock buybacks are often framed as value return to shareholders. But when insiders and the firm itself control a majority of the shares, the firm becomes its own most powerful voter — a closed loop of self-reinforcement.

This violates two core ALE principles:

- Logic, because it erases external feedback. (How can a system self-audit if it controls the audit?)

- Accountability, because power becomes untraceable. (Who decides? Who benefits?)

Governance Thresholds:

- If firm-held shares ≥ largest external shareholder: self-voting risk

- If (firm-held + executive-held) shares ≥ 50%: privatized governance

ALE Intervention:
Track the concentration of equity on the balance sheet. When ownership structures pass these thresholds, reclassify the firm as self-governing, and restrict eligibility for subsidies or tax incentives — since public benefit cannot be proven without public accountability.

3. Lobbying Offset Trigger (LOT): Bailouts Break Your Bullhorn

LOT introduces a conditional logic gate into corporate behavior:

If a firm receives public support (bailouts, subsidies, tax deferrals), it triggers a temporary ban on:

- Lobbying

- PAC participation

- Stock buybacks

Why?
Because you cannot simultaneously depend on public rescue and shape public policy. That's a direct violation of both equity (unearned influence) and accountability (misuse of subsidized advantage).

ALE Intervention:
Once LOT is triggered, the firm's financial disclosures must note that it is in a non-advocacy window, and

compensation policies must adjust accordingly (e.g., no bonuses tied to EPS inflation during this window).

This construct prevents firms from using public generosity as a platform for private gain.

4. Public Exposure Threshold (PET): A Line That Demands Accountability

PET establishes a red line in terms of systemic dependency. If a firm's public support crosses a given threshold — say, 20% or more of its profitability tied to externalized cost or public assistance — it triggers transparency or redistribution requirements.

Example triggers:

- 15% of workforce on public assistance

- 10%+ revenue tied to government contracts/subsidies

- Deferred environmental liabilities exceeding declared equity reserves

Once PET is crossed:

- The firm is subject to mandatory ALE evaluation

- Certain financial behaviors (buybacks, offshore reinvestment) are restricted

- A "public contribution" line item must appear on its balance sheet

Why it matters:
PET turns hidden reliance into a visible constraint, reinforcing the idea that when the public carries risk, the public earns a seat at the table.

Together, These Constructs Transform ALE Into a Governance System

Each of these tools — DD, RE, LOT, PET — represents a boundary. A place where philosophy becomes policy. A moment where ethics intervene on economics not through slogans, but through structure.

They do not punish firms for growing.
They challenge firms to grow with integrity.

And in doing so, they move us one step closer to a world where business doesn't just follow the numbers — it follows reason.

Example: Orion Logistics

To see how the ALE Standard functions in practice, consider the case of Orion Logistics, Inc.

Orion is a publicly celebrated company that touts:

- $2.3 billion in annual revenue

- $350 million in net income

- ESG recognition due to fleet electrification

- Executive bonuses totaling $60 million

- GAAP-compliant reporting and strong shareholder returns

Under traditional metrics, Orion appears healthy, innovative, and efficient. But when evaluated through ALE, a different story emerges — one of invisible dependencies, narrative-driven valuation, and systemic imbalance.

Accountable

- Orion received $120 million in government subsidies, unacknowledged in their balance sheet as structural support.

- 38% of Orion's workers qualify for public assistance — wages are suppressed, and the shortfall is externalized.

- Deferred liabilities from environmental waste and infrastructure wear are omitted entirely.

Fails Accountable. Profit is achieved through unacknowledged public scaffolding.

Logical

- "Brand goodwill" inflates asset values by $480 million, tied to speculative international expansion.

- Orion claims licensing revenue from routing software built in part on publicly funded research.

- Revenue is booked on advance carrier partnerships prior to delivery.

Fails Logical. The numbers compute, but the story does not follow causality.

Equitable

- Executive and shareholder gains are concentrated through buybacks while labor and communities absorb risk.

- Infrastructure — roads, utilities, broadband — is subsidized but not reinvested in.

- When local tax abatements expire, Orion relocates, leaving public partners with the costs.

Fails Equitable. The firm captures reward while displacing the cost onto others.

ALE Constructs Activated:

- **Depreciation Disparity (DD):** Capital assets are depreciated for tax advantage. Labor is not.

- **Recursive Equity (RE):** Executives and the firm itself own over 50% of voting shares — triggering governance failure.

- **Lobbying Offset Trigger (LOT):** Despite receiving public aid, Orion engaged in lobbying and stock buybacks within the same fiscal year.

- **Public Exposure Threshold (PET):** At least 15% of employees are on public assistance, and over 10% of revenue comes from government contracts. PET is crossed. ALE evaluation is required.

How to Interpret ALE Outputs

The ALE Standard is not a rating system. It is a logic and fairness audit — a way to identify where perception diverges from reality. When a firm is tested using ALE, the following outputs emerge:

- A pass/fail evaluation across all three pillars: Accountable, Logical, Equitable

- A modified balance sheet profile that incorporates hidden public contributions and risk displacement

- A diagnostic exposure of any governance thresholds violated via DD, RE, LOT, or PET

- Optional quantitative outputs such as an ALE Exposure Ratio — estimating how much of declared profit is derived from public subsidy, offloaded cost, or deferred liability

Interpretation is holistic. A firm may pass one or two dimensions, but consistent failure across all three — especially when combined with systemic constructs — reveals a business model grounded more in narrative than contribution.

ALE does not measure brand.
ALE measures alignment with truth.

What ALE Unveils

Conventional reporting celebrates performance.
It rewards momentum, compliance, and well-shaped narratives — treating financial coherence as self-evident if the statements balance and the story sells. But ALE does not celebrate stories. It interrogates them.

It does not ask whether the firm looks healthy.
It asks whether the health is real, and whether it was achieved at someone else's expense.

ALE pulls back the curtain on the modern economy — not as a machine of merit, but as a structure of selective visibility.

It reveals that:

- **Profit can be subsidized** without ever being disclosed as shared.

- **Valuation can be speculative**, inflated by anticipation rather than contribution.

- **Responsibility can be outsourced** — onto the public, onto workers, onto time itself.

- **Compliance does not mean coherence**, and passing legal thresholds does not mean meeting ethical ones.

These are not footnotes to capitalism.
They are the blueprint behind much of what we mistake for success.

What ALE unveils is not new corruption or sudden failure.
It reveals a pattern — quiet, consistent, institutional.

We see it in:

- Firms that suppress wages while their workers are fed by public programs.

- Companies that buy back stock not to share value, but to manufacture the appearance of growth.

- Market darlings that flourish by deferring their liabilities (environmental, social, financial) onto communities they no longer serve.

ALE does not single out these companies as outliers. It identifies them as examples of a broader pattern — organizations operating within a system that allows selective disclosure and structured ambiguity. Over time, that system has grown so familiar with telling a clean story that it often loses sight of what's been left out.

What ALE offers is clarity — not through moral judgment, but through measurable reasoning. It doesn't exist to criticize success. It exists to help determine whether that success is based on substance.

If we lose the ability to distinguish between real value and carefully presented performance, the system we're participating in stops functioning as an economy. It becomes something else — something that may look like progress but doesn't hold up to examination.

ALE is built to begin that examination. And it continues working even when the answers challenge what we assumed to be true.

Why Existing Metrics Fail

The issue with existing metrics isn't that they're inherently wrong. It's that they were never designed to see the full picture. Most financial and performance systems aren't built to question what value actually is. They're built to measure what's already being claimed.

These tools don't account for dependency. They track performance within a narrow frame, often assuming that what can be measured is what matters. Fairness is rarely evaluated. Instead, consistency is rewarded — even when the underlying assumptions are incomplete or outdated.

This is not accidental. It's structural.

GAAP, for example, is a rules-based system. It tells us whether a company has followed accepted procedures — not whether those procedures reflect the real-world impacts of the business. Price-to-earnings ratios convert investor expectations into company valuation. They measure confidence, not delivery. ESG scores, despite good intentions, are often self-reported and tend to reward language over practice. Even GDP, which is used to assess national progress, treats nearly all economic activity as positive — regardless of whether it's extractive, harmful, or merely shifting risk.

These tools are not neutral. They reflect the priorities and blind spots of the systems that built them. They reward visibility more than integrity, and presentation more than structure.

As a result, the current system often praises companies that offload risk to workers, governments, or the environment. It allows short-term financial strategies like stock buybacks and layoffs to boost key metrics without addressing long-term sustainability. Growth is frequently celebrated, even when it's driven by legal loopholes or financial engineering rather than actual value creation.

What's being rewarded in these moments is not truth. It's performance.

ALE does not aim to replace these metrics. It places them in context. It helps reveal what they ignore: the costs they externalize, the dependencies they mask, and the shared systems they rely on while appearing to stand alone.

If business is going to remain a credible part of the future, it needs to be evaluated on more than profitability. It needs to be evaluated on coherence. It needs tools that can test not just whether it earned revenue, but whether it earned trust.

ALE is one way to do that. It doesn't abandon accounting. It reclaims its purpose: to reflect reality, not just compliance. To help make financial systems understandable — and to help make success meaningful again.

Closing: Rebuilding the Ledger

The Corporate Welfare Equation introduced a difficult truth: that much of what we currently define as profit is built on costs the public absorbs but never sees. The ALE Standard extended that insight. It showed not just what's missing from financial reports, but why those omissions happen — and what it means when businesses meet legal requirements but fail basic logical tests.

Taken together, these frameworks begin to shift the role of business back toward its intended purpose. They move us away from performance-driven perception and back toward measurable contribution. They frame business not as a spectacle, but as a system that should be accountable to those who sustain it.

These tools allow us to ask clearer questions:

- Who actually creates the value a company claims?

- Who carries the risk?

- Who shapes the story, and who pays for its impact?

And, more fundamentally:

- What should we expect from a system that claims to serve the public good?

ALE does not ask companies to be flawless. It asks them to be accurate. It asks that businesses document what's real — not just what is technically defensible. It pushes for profit to reflect genuine output, not the manipulation of optics. And it treats the public not as a silent observer, but as an active stakeholder in every financial decision that carries social consequences.

Truth, when measured with care, creates trust. And trust is what makes long-term systems possible. Without it, no performance can hold the structure together.

At the same time, numbers are no longer the only way businesses shape their image. Narrative has become a form of capital. Marketing doesn't just support value — it often defines it. To understand how distortion begins before it ever reaches the ledger, we now need to look at the most powerful influence in modern business: marketing.

7 The Marketing Integrity Test

Long before a company records revenue or ships a product, it tells a story. In modern business, that story often determines whether the company succeeds. Marketing, once considered a support function, now plays a central role in how value is created, perceived, and maintained.

It influences everything from pricing to ethics. It shapes how innovation is communicated and how risk is concealed. It is often the first point of contact between an organization and the public — and increasingly, it defines the terms of that relationship.

This shift has made marketing one of the most powerful forces in the business world. In the absence of meaningful oversight, it has evolved from a tool of persuasion into a mechanism for narrative control. At its most extreme, it becomes a form of narrative arbitrage — where the appearance of value is packaged and sold independently of whether that value exists.

Marketing today is often used to justify prices before products are functional, to promote innovation before delivery, to brand ethics without corresponding behavior, and to project legitimacy before accountability has been established.

This is not an indictment of marketing itself. The problem lies in the incentives. There are few structural checks on how language is used in business communication, and even fewer tools to verify whether claims made in marketing materials are grounded in operational reality.

In a system where perception drives investment, trust, and valuation, marketing becomes a central point of leverage. When left unchecked, it enables companies to bypass scrutiny and manage impressions without consequence. In many cases, this has made marketing the most sophisticated source of distortion in the modern economy.

The Marketing Integrity Test (MIT) was created to bring structure back to this space. It provides a way to evaluate the relationship between what a company says and what it actually delivers. It allows us to test claims, trace promises, and assess whether marketing reflects truth or simply constructs it.

Without this kind of structure, the ledger cannot be trusted. Because no matter how precise the numbers are, they rely on the stories that come before them. And unless those stories are grounded in something real, everything that follows is built on unstable ground.

The Kickstarter Paradox

Picture a highly polished product video: soft music, clean visuals, and a confident founder explaining how a new device will change the way you cook, sleep, or focus. It doesn't just solve a problem — it promises to redefine an entire category.

There's just one issue. There's no working prototype. There's no manufacturing plan. There's no evidence the product is viable. But the presentation is flawless.

The campaign goes on to raise millions of dollars in less than a month.

By the time production stalls, refunds are delayed, and supporters begin voicing concern, the momentum has already done its job. The story succeeded — regardless of whether the product ever did.

This is the Kickstarter Paradox: a situation where narrative precedes production and is rewarded as if the value it implies already exists.

The concern isn't with crowdfunding itself. It's with a broader structural issue — the growing tendency to treat marketing as a substitute for proof. When story becomes more important than structure, and when persuasion is rewarded independently of performance, trust is replaced by traction.

While crowdfunding provides a clear, consumer-facing example, the same dynamic appears across other sectors:

- Startups that attract investment based on pitch decks rather than revenue

- Sustainability campaigns that conceal extractive operations

- Diversity pledges that are released before policies are in place

- "AI-powered" claims that describe tools with no original intelligence

In each of these cases, marketing is used to manufacture belief before any results exist to support it. It creates momentum, not merit — and once that momentum reaches a certain point, the belief becomes self-sustaining.

By the time the promises are tested, the story has already reshaped perception, secured funding, attracted media attention, or influenced public policy. The underlying product or strategy doesn't need to deliver — because the belief has already served its purpose.

This is the kind of distortion the Marketing Integrity Test is designed to identify. It exposes the risks that emerge when language is used to replace logic, when ethics are reduced to branding, and when communication is treated as a substitute for accountability.

If we fail to recognize how persuasive storytelling can override structural reasoning, we'll continue to confuse visibility for value — and reward systems that are designed to captivate rather than contribute.

Marketing as Distortion Engine

In a healthy market, value is earned through contribution. In a distorted one, value is implied through perception. Modern marketing is no longer just a way to communicate features or benefits — it has become a system for managing belief. And belief, when shaped early and strategically, can be converted into measurable value before any meaningful result is delivered.

This goes beyond communication. It functions more like currency.

We've moved away from a model where products are developed, tested, and then promoted. Increasingly, promotion comes first — and in many cases, it replaces production altogether.

In this environment, narrative serves as collateral. Aesthetic choices are treated as evidence. Confidence becomes a stand-in for capability.

Storytelling itself isn't new. What has changed is the boundary between telling a story and constructing a simulation. That line, in many parts of the business world, has quietly disappeared.

Marketing now serves as one of the most effective ways to bypass critical evaluation. It doesn't require logical coherence, only emotional resonance. It doesn't rely on independent verification, only repetition. It doesn't need accountability if it can reach a large enough audience.

Once belief takes hold, markets react — not to what's been built or delivered, but to what has been perceived. The momentum generated by that perception often carries more weight than the actual outcome.

This shift has disrupted the traditional feedback loop that once connected function with trust. Instead of evaluating long-term impact, many systems now reward initial impressions. And because those impressions are often shaped by design, narrative, or performance, it becomes difficult to tell whether something is complete — or simply presented that way.

The Figma Fallacy, Revisited

When the Figma Fallacy was first described, it appeared to be a design issue — an example of a prototype being mistaken for a functional product. A user interface, polished and interactive, could give the impression of readiness even when no underlying system had been built.

But this isn't just a flaw in how products are developed. It reflects a deeper logic at work in modern marketing.

The Figma Fallacy exists because our current business environment increasingly rewards presentation over proof. What begins as a design shortcut often becomes a business strategy. Mockups are treated as market signals. Pitch decks take the place of production plans. Demo videos shape valuation well before working code exists.

And it's not limited to product design.

We see it in early-stage startups raising capital without functional prototypes. We see it in ESG campaigns launched before internal policies are in place. We see it in AI tools promoted with exaggerated claims based on limited or highly curated outputs. Even traditional financial services firms now rebrand outdated offerings with "tech-forward" language to appear more innovative than they are.

This isn't just marketing hype — it's performance without production.

It allows companies to gain trust, raise capital, and earn credibility through narrative alone. In many cases, the appearance of value becomes more important than the delivery of it.

The Figma Fallacy, once a specific issue in product development, now illustrates a broader pattern across business: showing before building, selling before serving, and performing before proving. And in systems that reward belief, the illusion of readiness is often treated as equivalent to reality.

As long as the audience believes it's real, there's no immediate need for it to be.

Why Marketing Must Be Tested

Markets have never been defined by numbers alone. At their foundation, they represent a set of agreements — both explicit and implicit — between those who offer value and those who engage with that value in good faith.

When marketing becomes disconnected from delivery, that agreement begins to fall apart. In the absence of verification, language can be used to construct narratives that bear little resemblance to reality. Style begins to replace substance, and perception becomes the primary measure of success.

In this environment, a message does not need to be accurate. It only needs to be persuasive enough to gain traction before anyone has the opportunity — or incentive — to test it. The problem is not with creativity or ambition. The problem is that untested persuasion introduces a systemic vulnerability.

If markets reward claims simply because they are compelling or widely shared, without requiring evidence or accountability, the result is not innovation. It is distortion. When visibility becomes more valuable than accuracy, discernment erodes — and the consequences extend far beyond communication.

In that kind of system:

- Truth loses its relevance in competitive environments

- The public becomes a means to an end, rather than a stakeholder

- Trust, once earned, is repackaged and resold as a resource to be extracted

This is why marketing must be examined — not censored or suppressed, but evaluated with the same intellectual standards we apply to financial reporting, product safety, and ethical governance. Persuasion, like any powerful tool, must be accountable to the reality it claims to represent.

The Marketing Integrity Test is built on that premise. It recognizes that language — like capital — has influence, and that influence must be tested. In a system where belief can be monetized, storytelling carries responsibility. And that responsibility should be measured, not assumed.

When language moves faster than truth, we need tools that help realign them. MIT is one such tool. It doesn't diminish the role of narrative — it restores its credibility.

The Marketing Integrity Test (MIT) Formula

If the Corporate Welfare Equation (CWE) exposed how profit can be extracted from the public without acknowledgment...
And if the ALE Standard showed how financial coherence can be faked through selective accounting...
Then the Marketing Integrity Test addresses the force that precedes both:

The manipulation of perception before value is proven.

MIT does not ask whether a company sounds compelling. It asks whether the claims made through marketing align with what is ultimately delivered — to customers, to users, and to the public.

Because the problem isn't storytelling.
It's storytelling without substance.

At Its Core: A Truth-Value Ratio

The MIT evaluates marketing integrity through a simple formula:

$$M(C) = \frac{V_{\text{delivered}}}{V_{\text{communicated}}}$$

Where:

- $V_{\text{delivered}}$ = Verifiable value received by end users or the public

- $V_{\text{communicated}}$ = Value promised or projected through marketing

This ratio doesn't measure creativity, aesthetics, or tone. It measures alignment between messaging and reality. Between what was said and what was actually done.

It is the philosophical equivalent of a truth audit — a way to evaluate whether persuasion is being used to convey value, or to simulate it.

Just as the price-to-book ratio reflects the gap between market sentiment and financial fundamentals, the MIT reflects the gap between projected value and delivered value.

Interpreting MIT Values

- $M(C)=1$: **Marketing is accurate, honest, and aligned.** Value was communicated clearly and delivered as expected. No ethical concerns.

79

- $M(C)<1$: **Marketing overstated reality.** Claims exceeded actual delivery. This suggests distortion, manipulation, or narrative arbitrage.

- $M(C)>1$: **Marketing understated reality.** Rare, typically found in public interest organizations or ethical firms that deliver more than they promise.

MIT is not designed to punish optimism.
It is designed to flag systemic overstatement — especially when marketing is used to front-run production, inflate valuation, or bypass scrutiny.

When marketing creates more value than the product itself,
we are no longer selling function — we are selling fantasy.

And when that fantasy is monetized — through funding, stock price, policy favor, or public trust — the cost is no longer theoretical.

It is absorbed by:

- Customers who were misled

- Investors who were baited

- Communities who were promised impact that never came

MIT gives us a way to measure this cost — not in feelings, but in ratios.
Not as a moral judgment, but as a logical test.

Because when marketing becomes a product in itself, truth must become a standard.

The Ethical Gates of the Marketing Integrity Test

While the MIT formula quantifies the gap between value promised and value delivered, numerical alignment alone cannot fully capture the ethical integrity of a message. Marketing can cause harm not only through its content, but through its delivery — particularly when it exploits timing, emotional influence, or hidden imbalances in knowledge and power.

To account for these subtler failures, the MIT framework includes three binary Ethical Gates. These gates are not score modifiers; they are override mechanisms. If any one is triggered, the marketing is presumed ethically compromised unless the firm can provide compelling counter-evidence. Each gate represents a distinct logic-breaking mode of influence — one that often bypasses informed consent, suppresses scrutiny, or manufactures belief before there is a functioning reality to support it.

Gate 1: The Figma Fallacy

Has the firm marketed a product, feature, or service before it was functionally real or materially usable?

This is the foundational failure that prompted the development of the MIT. Named after the common use of polished mockups created in tools like Figma, the fallacy refers to instances where an incomplete or speculative product is presented as if it were launch-ready. These campaigns are often so visually compelling that they override questions of substance.

Common examples include software platforms marketed solely on the basis of UI animations, hardware products unveiled before supply chains or critical components are secured, and health-related products promoted before regulatory approval or clinical validation.

This kind of pre-functional marketing creates synthetic confidence. It simulates value that may never be delivered and monetizes belief before there is any evidence to support it. When the Figma Fallacy is triggered, the MIT score must be interpreted with heightened skepticism. The perceived value is likely fictional, and the consequences of that fiction can extend well beyond the company — harming users, misleading investors, and distorting public policy responses.

Gate 2: Behavioral Manipulation

Has the firm used urgency, scarcity, fear, or psychological leverage to accelerate adoption or suppress scrutiny?

This gate addresses influence strategies designed to override logical decision-making. Rather than presenting information for rational evaluation, these tactics appeal to emotional vulnerabilities — often exploiting fear of missing out or social pressure to act quickly.

Examples include campaigns driven by artificial scarcity, such as fake waitlists or staged "limited-time" offers that are never truly limited. They also include calls to action that use language like "act now or lose out," or frame hesitation as a personal failure, as seen in lines like "don't get left behind."

Behavioral manipulation distorts consent by reducing the space for critical thought. It pressures users into decisions they might not make with more time or information and often leads to premature or excessive adoption of immature technologies. This is particularly dangerous in sectors like finance, health, and surveillance, where the risks of over-adoption are more than speculative — they are structural.

Gate 3: Asymmetric Knowledge

Does the firm omit, obscure, or bury known risks to the user, public, or system at large?

This gate addresses the intentional use of complexity or omission to conceal known drawbacks. The tactic is not to lie, but to withhold — creating a false perception of safety or benefit through selective transparency.

Examples include marketing products while suppressing knowledge of side effects, monetizing user data without clear or informed consent, and using technical complexity to obscure how a product functions. This is common in AI and algorithmic systems where end users are asked to "trust the model" without having any access to its logic or limitations.

When this gate is triggered, marketing becomes a mechanism of power asymmetry. It reinforces the firm's ability to extract value from users while denying them the information needed to assess risks or exercise choice.

How These Gates Interact with M(C)

The ethical gates do not replace the MIT formula; they refine its interpretation. A company may score reasonably well using the core ratio — for example, a marketing claim may yield an M(C) score of 0.85. However, if any ethical gate is triggered, the discrepancy between communicated and delivered value is no longer considered benign. It is structural and intentional. The failure is not an oversight — it is a strategy.

When any gate is triggered, the following actions are recommended:

- The marketing should be categorized as manipulative, not merely imprecise.

- Disclosure requirements should increase, particularly in public-facing sectors.

- In regulated industries, gate-triggering campaigns may justify penalties, audit flags, or even the revocation of advertising privileges.

Marketing is not ethically neutral simply because it is persuasive or effective. When storytelling replaces verification, and narrative becomes a form of strategic simulation, marketing is no longer performing a communicative function. It becomes a systemic engine of distortion — and the harm it causes will not be limited to the firm that deployed it.

Example Applying the MIT to Orion Logistics

Orion Logistics is well known for its clean branding, confident leadership, and reputation as a "tech-forward" supply chain company. Its website claims it is "reinventing logistics through intelligent optimization," and its recent ad campaign positioned Orion as the "greenest fleet in North America."

The press coverage was glowing.
Investors were impressed.
Analysts raised their valuation targets.

But when we apply the Marketing Integrity Test, the story begins to unravel.

The MIT Score: $M(C) = 0.61$

Orion's marketing communicated value that far exceeded what was delivered:

- Its "proprietary AI engine" was later revealed to be a lightly modified open-source routing library.

- Its fleet electrification initiative was not in active deployment — it had secured grant funding, but no electric vehicles had been delivered or charged.

- Customer efficiency claims (e.g., "23% faster delivery times") were based on a small internal pilot, not scaled results.

The MIT truth-value ratio reflected this gap:
Out of the total value projected by marketing, only 61% had been substantiated by product performance or operational outcomes.

This alone raises ethical concerns. But the gates tell the deeper story.

Gate 1: The Figma Fallacy — Triggered

Orion marketed features and operational capabilities that did not yet exist in production.
It showcased an interactive UI demo of its "AI dashboard" in press videos, implying real-time tracking and dynamic routing powered by machine learning. Internally, the product was still undergoing early beta testing and lacked full backend integration.

This wasn't vaporware in a malicious sense — it was presentation-first development. But the effect was the same: customers, journalists, and investors were given the impression of maturity where there was none.

Gate 2: Behavioral Manipulation — Triggered

Orion's landing pages used a countdown timer urging enterprise customers to "sign up by Friday" to receive

85

early access pricing.
The timer reset every 24 hours.

Their email campaign used phrases like "Don't be left behind in a carbon-neutral future" and "Your competitors are already saving — are you?" These appeals were designed to pressure conversion, not inform.

The strategy wasn't illegal. But it bypassed reasoned evaluation by creating urgency from a position of incomplete delivery.

Gate 3: Asymmetric Knowledge — Triggered

Internal reports at Orion acknowledged that the majority of its carbon reduction claims were based on forecasted performance, not verified emissions reductions.
This detail was absent from its ESG marketing and sustainability brochures. In other words, the company had access to information that would materially change how stakeholders perceived its environmental impact — and it chose not to disclose it.

This is a textbook case of asymmetric knowledge: not lying outright, but selectively omitting known risks and caveats to maintain a polished public narrative.

Interpretation

On paper, Orion scored a 0.61 on the MIT scale — already a red flag for exaggerated claims. But the triggering of all three ethical gates elevates the concern from marketing misalignment to structured manipulation.

It suggests that Orion is not simply communicating aspirational value. It is constructing a belief environment that substitutes for delivery — while externalizing the risks of that belief onto users, investors, and the public.

In a regulatory context, this would justify:

- Increased disclosure requirements

- Restrictions on public marketing until delivery aligns with claim

- Potential civil penalties if harm arises from reliance on false confidence (e.g., investor losses, contract disputes)

How to Interpret MIT Results

The Marketing Integrity Test (MIT) produces more than a number. It generates a profile of alignment and influence, revealing whether a firm's narrative is anchored in substance — or constructed for effect.

While the M(C) ratio quantifies the gap between value communicated and value delivered, its true interpretive strength emerges when read in concert with the ethical gate triggers.

Together, they provide a comprehensive diagnostic:

M(C) = 1.0

Interpretation: The firm's marketing is fully aligned with what it delivers. Claims are substantiated, expectations are met, and communication reflects operational reality. Ethical risk is minimal.

Recommended classification: *Credible, responsible communication.*

M(C) = 0.85–0.99

Interpretation: Minor overstatements are present — often aspirational in nature — but do not materially mislead. Marketing may lean into optimism, but delivery tracks closely enough to maintain trust.

Recommended classification: *Generally ethical marketing with modest exaggeration.*

Caution: If paired with an ethical gate trigger, the discrepancy should be treated as structured distortion, not minor enthusiasm.

$M(C) = 0.65–0.84$

Interpretation: Marketing overstates the company's capabilities or impact in a manner that may affect customer or investor decisions. The firm appears to rely on storytelling to sustain momentum before results are mature.

Recommended classification: *Misleading marketing, moderate ethical risk.*

Actionable flags: Evaluate whether urgency, ambiguity, or omission is driving belief. Check for Figma Fallacy or Behavioral Manipulation gate triggers.

$M(C) < 0.65$

Interpretation: There is a significant misalignment between narrative and delivery. The campaign likely prioritizes attention, valuation, or hype over truth. Ethical gates are often triggered in this range.

Recommended classification: *Manipulative marketing with systemic risk.*

Policy recommendation: Trigger audit, public transparency response, or regulatory review — especially if public trust, capital, or safety is at stake.

Ethical Gate Modifiers

Ethical gates sharpen the meaning of the M(C) score. Their presence changes how the result should be interpreted — not just as numerical misalignment, but as intentional distortion.

- If any gate is triggered, the MIT score must be treated as structurally compromised.

- If multiple gates are triggered, the campaign should be flagged as manipulative by design, not by accident.

- If no gates are triggered but the score is below 1.0, interpretation depends on industry norms, product maturity, and communication style.

Operational Use

Firms can use the MIT to audit their own campaigns pre-launch, ensuring that language, visuals, and claims track with reality. Investors and analysts can use the score and gate triggers as early indicators of reputational or valuation risk. Policy makers and oversight bodies can use MIT as a first-line filter for heightened review or advertising restrictions, especially in high-risk sectors.

Ultimately, the MIT reframes marketing from a soft skill to a structured system of influence.
And systems of influence, if left unchecked, don't just mislead markets —
They undermine trust itself.

What MIT Unveils

Most business frameworks treat marketing as a benign input — an accelerant for growth, a storytelling tool, a way to frame benefits for the audience. In theory, marketing is simply communication.

But the Marketing Integrity Test reveals a more complex truth.

MIT shows that in the modern economy, marketing is no longer just a reflection of value. It is often a substitute for it.

It unveils that:

- Perception is being monetized before performance exists.

- Belief is treated as a business asset — even when it's unearned.

- Language has been engineered to bypass logic, not support it.

MIT pulls into focus the fact that storytelling can now:

- Inflate valuations before infrastructure is built

- Guide public policy with no grounding in data

- Justify spending, regulation, or procurement based on traction, not trust

The issue is not that exaggeration exists. The issue is that the line between optimism and simulation has disappeared.
And when that happens, value becomes performative —

shaped by headlines, hype cycles, and high-conversion copy rather than substance.

Marketing, in this environment, becomes a meta-product: something sold not to explain the business, but to become the business.

MIT reveals:

- Companies that advertise sustainability before greening a single process

- Tech startups that sell access to platforms that don't yet function

- Financial services that promise democratization while obscuring risk

- Healthcare firms that deploy emotional storytelling while bypassing clinical disclosure

It shows that narrative has become a commodity — and one that can be far more profitable than the thing it supposedly represents.

This is not a superficial flaw.
It's a systemic blind spot that:

- Corrodes trust

- Misguides investment

- Distorts public perception of innovation, safety, and progress

MIT gives us a way to expose this pattern.
It reveals not only where alignment breaks down — but how firms use language to make the break appear invisible.

And it gives us a framework to say:
If a firm is selling a vision before it has built the foundation,
if belief has become the product,
and if marketing is its delivery mechanism,
then what's being sold is not a solution —
It's a story.

Why Existing Regulations Fall Short

Marketing is not entirely unregulated. In most countries, oversight exists in the form of advertising standards, consumer protection laws, and truth-in-advertising regulations. In the U.S., agencies like the Federal Trade Commission (FTC) require that marketing be truthful, non-deceptive, and evidence-based. The European Union enforces similar standards through consumer protection directives.

However, these frameworks suffer from three core limitations:

1. They respond to harm after the fact.
   Most regulatory action is reactive, triggered by consumer complaints, whistleblowers, or public scandals. By the time enforcement begins, the damage has already been done.

2. They focus on content, not context.
   Regulatory frameworks assess whether a specific claim is misleading or factually incorrect. They do not evaluate how marketing is structured to create belief independent of delivery, nor do they interrogate patterned omissions, emotional manipulation, or systemic misalignment.

3. They ignore philosophical coherence.
   Legal standards ask: "Is this provably false?" The
   MIT asks a deeper question: "Is this structurally
   honest?" That includes whether the message is
   testable, proportional, and accountable, even if it
   does not contain an outright lie.

In an era where entire business models are driven by
marketing momentum, these gaps are no longer technical
— they are structural.

The MIT does not replace regulatory tools.
It provides what they currently lack: a logic-based, values-
rooted framework for evaluating how marketing shapes
belief in ways that bypass accountability.

Closing: Why Marketing Must Be Measured

Marketing has always shaped perception. But in the
modern economy, it increasingly defines value before
value exists. This shift — quiet, systemic, and largely
unexamined — has allowed marketing to evolve from a
communication tool into a primary driver of belief,
investment, and strategic direction.

The Marketing Integrity Test restores structure to that
influence. It introduces a clear standard: that claims must
be proportional, testable, and accountable — and that
when they are not, the narrative must be treated as
suspect, not symbolic.

By measuring the gap between value communicated and
value delivered, and applying the ethical gates that reveal
where persuasion becomes distortion, MIT offers a way
to hold language accountable to reality.

This is not about restricting storytelling. It's about protecting the systems that depend on truth. The economy. The public. The commons.

With CWE, we examined how companies extract value from the public without acknowledgment.
With ALE, we tested the internal coherence of what is reported as value.
With MIT, we now confront how companies shape belief in that value — before it exists, and sometimes without ever intending to build it.

What follows is not just a conclusion.
It is a convergence.

Because once we see how marketing, accounting, and profit interact — once we understand how each can be used to simulate integrity while bypassing substance — we gain the ability to measure value more honestly, and rebuild trust on firmer ground.

8   The Market Integrity Equation

There was a time when value was tethered to output. A company's worth (whether private or public) rested on what it produced, how it served, and the role it played in meeting real human or economic need. The price of a business reflected something concrete: the machines it operated, the people it employed, the problems it solved.

But that linkage has been eroded.

Today, market valuation increasingly reflects narrative positioning, platform potential, and perception at scale. Entire industries have been built not on what they deliver, but on how well they are believed. Story has overtaken structure. Belief has become capital.

Speculation, once the outer layer of the market, is now embedded at the core.

And as the relationship between contribution and valuation continues to break down, so too does the ability of markets to signal anything coherent — about impact, about value, or about integrity.

This chapter is not an argument against markets.
It is a recognition that if markets are to remain credible, they must be measurable — not only in terms of growth, but in terms of grounding.

This is where the Market Integrity Equation enters. It offers a way to test whether a firm's valuation reflects something real — or merely something well-performed.

In the chapters before this, we examined how firms extract uncounted value from the public (CWE), distort internal narratives through compliant but incoherent reporting (ALE), and amplify synthetic belief through marketing (MIT). Each of these distortions moves capital — but none of them asks whether the capital is meaningfully anchored.

The Market Integrity Equation does.
Where CWE tracks extraction,
ALE tracks coherence,
MIT tracks influence —
MIE tracks belief.

It completes the ecosystem by answering the question:
Is this price connected to actual contribution — or are we rewarding performance without production?

Before we can restore trust in markets, we must be able to test what markets reward.

Market systems have always been influenced by speculation. But what once functioned as a margin of flexibility — a space where investors weighed risk and potential — has now become the central engine of valuation.

Firms are no longer measured by what they do.
They are measured by how much belief they can accumulate.

This shift didn't happen all at once. It emerged through successive innovations in financialization, branding, and market signaling. As software firms abstracted their operations, valuations became increasingly tied to future possibilities, not present outcomes. Marketing campaigns framed roadmap features as launch-ready. Founders were advised to "build in public," but what they really built was traction in advance of substance.

Eventually, entire business models were optimized not for delivery, but for investor psychology.

We now inhabit a system where:

- A pre-revenue startup can be valued in the billions.

- A company can announce layoffs and watch its stock rise.

- A firm's market cap can grow even as its output shrinks.

These are not outliers. They are features of a system that has made belief its most valuable commodity.

The market no longer tests contribution — it anticipates confidence.
It no longer asks what a firm creates — it asks how well it performs inevitability.

This is not simply a distortion of financial logic.
It is a philosophical breakdown. A shift from epistemology to ideology, where perception becomes truth and valuation becomes its own justification.

The consequence is that price no longer reflects value. It reflects visibility, velocity, and volume of narrative.

And if price becomes untethered from contribution, then markets cease to be markets.
They become myth systems — economies of belief, governed not by evidence, but by consensus perception.

To repair that disconnect, we must first make it visible.

That is the purpose of the Market Integrity Equation: not to devalue ambition, but to measure whether belief is being rewarded before it is earned.

The Valuation Mirage

One of the most dangerous distortions in the modern market is not fraud. It's coherence.
A firm's valuation can be entirely defensible within the rules of financial modeling, investment logic, and market momentum — while remaining completely detached from reality.

This is the Valuation Mirage: a condition where confidence compounds without correction.

It often begins with a promising idea. A product with clear potential. A founding team with pedigree. Early marketing generates interest. Early interest draws in capital. Capital creates headlines. Headlines generate social proof. Social proof accelerates demand.

At no point in this cycle does anyone need to ask:
Has the product scaled?
Has the impact materialized?
Has the contribution justified the price?

Because in a valuation mirage, price is not driven by delivery. It is driven by belief in future belief.

Each round of funding validates the last.
Each headline validates the valuation.
Each valuation validates the perception of inevitability.

Eventually, the firm is treated as successful — not because it has delivered value, but because it has maintained belief long enough to be declared viable.

This pattern is most common in speculative markets — technology, crypto, fintech — but it is no longer confined to them. Even legacy industries now lean into this cycle, reshaping earnings calls, branding, and investor decks to sustain visibility over performance.

The consequence is structural. When enough firms rely on this momentum loop to sustain valuation, markets stop rewarding production altogether. They reward the maintenance of illusion.

And unlike traditional bubbles, which pop visibly and painfully, valuation mirages often dissipate quietly — through delayed rollouts, missed projections, or quiet restatements that never make headlines.

The damage is cumulative.
Trust erodes.
Signal disappears.
Markets stop functioning as instruments of value and begin functioning as instruments of speculative mythology.

The Market Integrity Equation was designed to reveal when this pattern is in motion — not through sentiment analysis or investor opinion, but through a simple philosophical question:
What has been delivered, and does the price reflect it?

The Market Integrity Equation (MIE)

MIE is structured as a logical ratio:

$$\text{MIE} = \frac{V_{Real}}{V_{Traded}}$$

Where:

- V_{Real} = Verifiable productive output or social utility

- V_{Traded} = Prevailing market valuation of an asset, firm, or sector

When **MIE < 1**, the model identifies a valuation gap that may indicate:

- Inflated pricing

- Systemic narrative distortion

- Liquidity-based manipulation

- Market signals divorced from measurable contribution

This framework establishes ethical gating criteria — including:

- **Speculative Primacy (SPG)**

- **Liquidity Distortion (LDG)**

- **Access Asymmetry (AAG)**

Deriving V_{Real} and V_{Traded}

V_{Real} (Numerator):

- Derived from public filings, operating income, public use-value multipliers, and real-world impact.

- Adjustments can be made for:

    o Underpaid labor

    o Infrastructure contributions

    o Environmental or social value

V_{Traded} (Denominator):

- Derived from:

    o Market cap

    o Price-to-earnings or price-to-sales ratios

    o Valuations in private rounds or public offerings

    o Unrealized appreciation of tradable assets

Example: Applying the MIE to Orion Logistics

At first glance, Orion Logistics looks like a market success story.

The company has raised over $800 million across five funding rounds. Its valuation crossed $4.2 billion in its most recent Series D. Press coverage has framed it as a "supply chain disruptor." Its CEO is a regular presence on innovation panels and LinkedIn influencer lists.

Investors praise its potential to "revolutionize freight analytics through AI."

But beneath the headlines, Orion's actual output tells a different story.

- Its core routing product is still in pilot across less than 4% of its contracted carriers.

- Half of its revenue comes from reseller partnerships, not proprietary infrastructure.

- Most of its "AI" functionality is based on third-party software stitched together with minimal internal IP.

- The company has posted negative operating margins for eight consecutive quarters.

MIE Evaluation:

- V_{Traded} = $4.2 billion valuation based on venture funding and secondary market estimates

- V_{Real} = Estimated $280 million in real, recurring contribution (infrastructure value, wages, software delivery, and public logistics efficiency improvements)

$$\text{MIE}_{\text{Orion}} = \frac{280M}{4.2B} = 0.067$$

This is a significant red flag. While hype has carried the company far, its market valuation exceeds real-world contribution by a factor of nearly 15.

Ethical Gate Assessment:

- **SPG (Speculative Primacy):** Triggered
  Orion's price is built on expected disruption, not actual performance. Most media coverage highlights future use cases rather than proven outcomes.

- **LDG (Liquidity Distortion):** Triggered
  Orion has executed three internal share buybacks and restricted employee share liquidity to drive up perceived demand ahead of its planned IPO.

- **AAG (Access Asymmetry):** Triggered
  Early investors sold a portion of their equity during the last round at a 30% markup before financial statements showed slowing growth.

Conclusion:

Despite appearing "well-positioned," Orion fails all three ethical gates under MIE. It is not simply overvalued — it is structurally dishonest. The firm is performing confidence at scale, while contribution lags far behind.

How to Interpret MIE Outputs

The Market Integrity Equation is not a valuation tool — it is a reality check. It does not forecast price, assess growth potential, or simulate investor returns. It simply asks: Does the value assigned by markets reflect the value contributed to the world?

While capital markets are inherently forward-looking, there is a threshold beyond which optimism becomes substitution — where expected potential begins to replace actual production. The MIE score helps identify that threshold.

It functions as a logic test, not a financial opinion:

$MIE = 1$

Interpretation:
The firm's market valuation is aligned with its measurable output. Confidence reflects real performance, and capital is rewarding actual contribution. No ethical gating is triggered.

Status:
Grounded and coherent. The market signal reflects reality.

$MIE < 1$

Interpretation:
Market valuation exceeds real-world output. The asset is priced for belief, not delivery. The lower the score, the greater the degree of speculative inflation, narrative primacy, or engineered distortion.

Status:
Incoherent. Belief is displacing substance.
Gating required.

$MIE > 1$

Interpretation:
The firm is undervalued. Its contribution to public, social, or economic systems exceeds what is currently priced in. These are often overlooked or underhyped firms that have not yet attracted investor attention or public visibility.

Status:

Unrecognized potential. Underappreciated or misaligned narrative. May represent a *moral blind spot* in the market, especially in cases of high utility but low investor return (e.g., worker-owned co-ops, public-benefit infrastructure, etc.).

MIE is sector-agnostic. It can be applied to individual firms, industries, or entire indexes. It does not require perfect data, but it demands consistency of logic — that belief must be anchored in something measurable, and price must pass a basic test of coherence.

Where traditional financial metrics reward growth and risk, MIE rewards reality.

MIE Value	Interpretation
MIE = 1	Market valuation reflects real output. No distortion.
MIE < 1	Traded value exceeds real output. Market is inflated by perception.
MIE > 1	Undervalued asset or firm. Real output is not yet recognized or rewarded by markets.

Ethical Gating System: When MIE < 1 Isn't an Accident

A low MIE score signals a disconnect between value and valuation. But not all disconnects are created equal. Some reflect market lag. Others reflect intentional distortion.

That's why the Market Integrity Equation includes three binary ethical gates — each designed to test whether the inflation of price is accidental, speculative, or engineered.

If any gate is triggered in tandem with MIE < 1, the firm's valuation should be considered structurally dishonest or extractive.

These are not subjective red flags. Each gate tests a specific violation of logical fairness, designed to expose the architecture of distortion that props up modern market narratives.

Gate 1: Speculative Primacy (SPG)

Test: Does valuation rely primarily on future returns or narrative hype?

Modern firms are increasingly priced for *what they might become*, rather than *what they currently are*. Forecasted dominance, total addressable market, or industry disruption become valuation inputs, even when no supporting performance exists.

This is speculative primacy: when expected value becomes a substitute for delivered value.

Examples:

- Pre-revenue tech startups with billion-dollar valuations

- Crypto assets with market caps driven by whitepapers, not function

- "Pre-product" companies priced for market capture that hasn't started

Why this matters:

When speculation replaces delivery, capital flows away from real production and into narrative engineering. This rewards firms that are best at *performing inevitability* — not building impact.

Failing SPG signals:
Narrative distortion. The firm is priced for belief, not delivery.

Gate 2: Liquidity Distortion (LDG)

Test: Has the asset been inflated via buybacks, financial engineering, or synthetic scarcity?

In a liquidity-distorted environment, price signals are not emergent — they are manufactured. Executives may reduce public float to spike share price. Tokens may be locked to inflate crypto valuations. Private firms may restrict share offerings to simulate demand.

This is liquidity distortion: where valuation is manipulated by supply control, not market consensus.

Examples:

- Share buybacks used to drive earnings-per-share and executive bonuses

- Crypto coins where a majority of supply is held by insiders

- Private equity "marking up" internal valuations based on limited trades

Why this matters:

Markets depend on liquidity to test value. When liquidity is controlled, truth becomes a casualty of scarcity theater.

Failing LDG signals:
Financial manipulation. Price is detached from open market behavior.

Gate 3: Access Asymmetry (AAG)

Test: Do insiders disproportionately benefit via structural or informational advantage?

Some market actors operate with privileged access: early entry to investment rounds, algorithmic trading advantages, or knowledge of internal metrics. These insiders can extract returns before the public has enough information to make informed decisions.

This is access asymmetry: when valuation serves the informed, not the invested.

Examples:

- Founders cashing out via SPACs or IPOs before performance is proven

- Private data used to front-run trades or structure buyouts

- Early investors offloading at inflated prices to later-stage retail buyers

Why this matters:

When insiders benefit from privileged access while others absorb the risk, markets don't just become unfair — they become untrustworthy.

Failing AAG signals:
Power imbalance. Value is captured without risk or contribution.

When to Apply the Gates

Gates are only activated when MIE < 1, but when triggered, they transform interpretation. They move the diagnosis from:

"The market is optimistic,"
to:
"The market is complicit in distortion."

And when multiple gates are triggered?
That's not just market exuberance. That's systemic narrative laundering.

Gate	Name	Test	Failing Condition
SPG	Speculative Primacy Gate	Does valuation rely primarily on expected future returns or narrative hype?	Yes
LDG	Liquidity Distortion Gate	Has the firm or asset been inflated via buybacks or engineered scarcity?	Yes
AAG	Access Asymmetry Gate	Do insiders benefit disproportionately via information or structural advantage?	Yes

Theoretical Basis

MIE builds on:

- Use-value (Marx) vs. exchange-value distinction
- Narrative contagion (Shiller) as a market force

- Economic realism: If valuation doesn't map to contribution, it's fiction.

It places markets in the realm of testable logics, rather than mythic systems of divine allocation.

What MIE Unveils

Where conventional metrics celebrate momentum, MIE interrogates foundation.

It forces a confrontation with the uncomfortable truth: that much of what is praised as market performance is built not on contribution, but on anticipation. MIE makes visible the distortions we've normalized — those that operate quietly beneath the surface of valuation.

It reveals that:

- Valuation can grow independent of delivery

- Narratives can become self-reinforcing financial assets

- Liquidity and access are not neutral — they shape who benefits and who bears risk

MIE gives language to patterns we've long sensed but struggled to name:

- That certain firms are rewarded for confidence, not competence

- That synthetic scarcity and insider advantage masquerade as organic success

- That public trust in markets erodes not from crashes — but from the quiet decay of coherence

It reorients market analysis around a forgotten principle:
Price must mean something.
If it does not map to output, it is not a signal — it's a story.

And when enough firms succeed by story alone, capital is no longer an enabler of innovation.
It becomes a system of speculative extraction — a race to monetize belief before reality catches up.

MIE doesn't fix that on its own.
But it gives us the tools to test it, expose it, and name it.
And that's where reform begins.

Fair Market Evaluation Test (FMET)

A Logic-Based Rubric for Grounded Valuation Assessment

Purpose

While the Market Integrity Equation (MIE) exposes valuation distortion by comparing real productive value to traded market value, some firms — like Costco — present an important edge case. They may have a low MIE not due to extractive behavior, but because the market systematically undervalues steady, utility-based contributions.

The Fair Market Evaluation Test (FMET) provides a companion logic tool to assess whether a firm with a low MIE is underappreciated or extractive. It helps distinguish between companies whose valuations reflect real, grounded contribution and those inflated by perception, hype, or financial manipulation.

Framework

Let:

- U = **Use-Value** (real-world benefit to consumers, access equity)

- E_P = **Employee Participation** (wage fairness, stability, retention)

- P_S = **Pricing Stability** (resistance to inflation or volatility)

- R_L = **Revenue Loyalty** (repeat engagement, low churn, high trust)

- F_E = **Financial Engineering** (buybacks, equity distortion, EPS targeting)

- V_M = **Market Valuation**

Core Logic Test

If $(U + E_P + P_S + R_L) > F_E$, then V_M is logically grounded

If $F_E > (U + E_P + P_S + R_L)$, then V_M is artificially inflated

This structure mirrors ethical reasoning found in distributive justice: if the benefit to stakeholders outweighs internal manipulation, valuation may exceed MIE but retain legitimacy.

Application: Costco

Component	Qualitative Score	Justification
U	High	Tangible goods, member pricing, household essentials
E_P	High	Equitable wages, low turnover, internal promotion
P_S	High	Maintains consistent prices during supply shocks
R_L	Very High	90%+ member renewal across decades
F_E	Low	Minimal buybacks, low debt, transparent books

Interpretation:

$$(U + E_P + P_S + R_L) \gg F_E \Rightarrow V_M \text{ is justifiable}$$

Costco's valuation is not a product of speculative hype but of scaled trust and real contribution — exactly what markets should reward but rarely do.

Why FMET Exists — and What It Reveals

FMET may be seen as a corrective. A failsafe. A way to protect high-integrity firms from being mislabeled as overvalued by a system that prizes spectacle.

But its very existence signals something deeper:

If value must be defended, then valuation is broken.

In a healthy market, firms like Costco — those that deliver real goods, pay workers well, maintain trust across decades — should be held up as benchmarks of economic success. But because they do not manufacture hype, dilute shares for profit, or inflate earnings through engineered scarcity, they often lag behind in perception.

The Market Integrity Equation exposes that gap. FMET explains why it exists — and why the failure is not in the company, but in the system.

In this way, FMET does more than just rescue firms from misclassification. It shows us what a justifiable valuation actually looks like:

- One grounded in use-value

- One bolstered by equitable internal practices

- One that resists distortion

- One that earns loyalty over time — not through marketing, but through meaning

And when you see how rare that pattern is in modern markets, FMET becomes more than a logic gate. It becomes a mirror — showing us how far we've drifted from the principles we claim to uphold.

FMET doesn't just protect firms from market blindness. It reminds us that real value doesn't need amplification — it needs recognition.

Why Existing Metrics Fail

Traditional valuation metrics were never designed to test fairness. They were built to price risk, project returns, and compare investor opportunity — not to interrogate whether value creation was real, shared, or sustainable.

They measure what markets reward.
They do not question whether markets reward the right things.

- Price-to-Earnings (P/E) rewards engineered scarcity and profit concentration.

- Earnings Per Share (EPS) is easily distorted through stock buybacks and cost shifting.

- Discounted Cash Flow (DCF) inflates projections through aggressive assumptions, turning hope into value.

- EBITDA conveniently omits the cost of debt, taxes, and reinvestment — core burdens that define sustainability.

- Even Total Shareholder Return assumes shareholders are the only constituency that matters.

Each metric contains embedded assumptions — that profit is merit, growth is virtue, and the future can be priced like a spreadsheet.

But none of them ask:

- Who benefits from this performance?

- Who pays for the growth that's being celebrated?

- Is this value, or is it momentum dressed as substance?

In an age of narrative-driven investing, financial engineering, and soft monopolies, these metrics no longer test reality. They validate illusion. And in doing so, they mask harm, misprice risk, and normalize distortion as success.

That's why MIE was created: not to compete with traditional models, but to ask the question they forgot to include:

Does this valuation reflect actual contribution — or just the performance of inevitability?

And it's why FMET must exist alongside it:
Because even when markets undervalue honesty, coherence, and shared prosperity — we don't have to.

The Path Back to Coherence

The Market Integrity Equation and Fair Market Evaluation Test were developed in response to a structural problem: traditional market metrics no longer distinguish between hype and contribution. They reflect momentum more than merit, and reinforce systems that reward perception over production.

MIE addresses this directly. It compares what firms deliver against what they are worth in the eyes of investors, using a simple ratio to test coherence between price and value. When the ratio is low, it raises a fundamental concern: has belief overtaken substance?

FMET expands this analysis. It protects firms that contribute meaningfully to the economy but fail to match the storytelling power of their competitors. In doing so, it reminds us that under-valuation can be just as misleading as inflation — especially when it obscures systems that function ethically and equitably.

Together, these tools offer a new approach to valuation. Not by replacing financial models, but by testing their assumptions. They reintroduce logic where momentum has displaced it. And they help policymakers, fiduciaries, and the public evaluate markets with clarity, not just confidence.

This chapter is not a rejection of investment, innovation, or growth. It is a call to recognize the difference between economic progress and financial abstraction — and to reward the former with structure that reflects its value.

9   So What Now?

By now, the patterns are no longer subtle. What once seemed like isolated flaws — misleading marketing, overinflated valuations, hollow financials — have revealed themselves as systemic distortions. And more importantly, they've revealed that the system as a whole lacks a coherent way to test itself.

That's why these frameworks were built — not to expose failure for its own sake, but to give structure back to scrutiny.

Each test in this book isolates a specific type of failure:

- **CWE** reveals when private profit is built on public burden.

- **ALE** tests whether internal reporting reflects reality or performance.

- **MIT** measures whether marketing matches delivery — or manufactures belief.

- **MIE** assesses whether a firm's valuation is grounded in contribution or inflated by narrative.

- **FMET** accounts for under-recognized value in firms that resist hype but operate ethically.

Each framework offers a focused perspective on a specific kind of distortion. On its own, it highlights one area where economic logic or ethical structure has broken down. But when viewed together, they don't just provide isolated insights — they function as a unified system.

Rather than reacting to headlines or relying on instinct, this system enables structured analysis. It replaces conjecture with logic. Where spin and narrative once dominated, it reintroduces clarity and structure.

Most importantly, these tools allow for the restoration of coherence — across markets, policy, and our understanding of value itself. Without that structure, we don't just risk mispricing assets. We risk eroding public trust and making decisions based on perception rather than truth.

This chapter is not about introducing new concepts. It's about integrating the ones already presented — demonstrating how they reinforce one another and serve as a framework for accountability, not just analysis.

A System of Tests: How the Frameworks Interact

The five frameworks introduced throughout this book were not designed to compete with existing models, but to complement and correct them. Each addresses a different form of distortion — whether it's extraction, manipulation, misalignment, or under-recognition. Together, they function as a modular system. Applied individually, they flag failure. Applied together, they form a coherent infrastructure of integrity.

Below is a summary of how each framework functions:

Framework	Primary Focus	What It Tests	Fails When...	Core Value Defended
CWE	Public burden	Net public impact	A company extracts more than it contributes	Reciprocity
ALE	Financial coherence	Internal consistency	Compliance masks	Logic

Framework	Primary Focus	What It Tests	Fails When...	Core Value Defended
		of financial reports	contradiction or omission	
MIT	Narrative alignment	Match between marketing and delivery	Belief is manufactured before delivery	Consent
MIE	Market valuation	Real output vs. traded value	Valuation exceeds contribution	Price integrity
FMET	Undervalued ethics	Social utility + moral footprint	Ethical value is ignored or underpriced	Recognition

This table isn't just a reference — it's a map. Each framework speaks to a different system failure, but they also complement one another:

- ALE captures what CWE misses when financial statements appear legitimate but still obscure public cost.

- MIT catches value inflation when ALE shows compliance and CWE isn't triggered.

- MIE builds on both, exposing how markets reward belief over delivery.

- FMET ensures the system isn't blind to firms that do good work without theatrical scale.

When applied together, the frameworks allow us to diagnose complexity without oversimplifying — and to

121

test performance not only through outcomes, but through structure, reasoning, and ethical coherence.

Case Study: Theranos

A Complete System Failure

Few companies illustrate structural failure more comprehensively than Theranos. At its peak, the company was valued at nearly $10 billion, despite having no fully functional product, a concealed revenue model, and deeply misleading public communications. While Theranos is now defunct, it serves as a cautionary example of what happens when every test of business integrity is bypassed or broken.

When viewed through the combined lens of CWE, ALE, MIT, MIE, and FMET, Theranos does not simply represent a failed startup — it represents the collapse of structure in every layer of ethical accountability.

Corporate Welfare Equation (CWE)

$$CWE = \frac{\text{Public Burden} - \text{Public Return}}{\text{Public Return}}$$

$$= \frac{\$250M \text{ (reputational, regulatory, and systemic burden)} - \$0}{\$0}$$

Test: Did the firm extract more from public systems than it returned?

Theranos leveraged the prestige of partnerships with Walgreens, Safeway, and public health institutions to gain credibility and secure valuation growth. It positioned itself as a disruptor in healthcare — an industry inherently linked to public trust and taxpayer-funded oversight.

Yet the benefits were largely asymmetric. The company:

- Took advantage of regulatory blind spots for laboratory-developed tests (LDTs)

- Delayed detection of false results, creating public health risks

- Used military and humanitarian health promises in marketing without delivering

CWE is undefined numerically due to a zero return, but in practice, the outcome is clear: public cost with no measurable return.

CWE Result: Negative public ROI. The firm extracted credibility and legitimacy from public systems without returning tangible public value.

ALE Standard

No numeric formula — pass/fail based on three tests

Test: Did the firm's financial statements reflect accountability, logic, and equity?

Theranos routinely overstated revenue projections and selectively presented performance data to investors. Internally, it used opaque accounting practices that masked operational losses and technical setbacks.

- In 2014, it claimed projected revenue of $100 million; actual revenue was approximately $100,000

- It created a "community-adjusted" narrative similar to WeWork's misleading EBITDA logic

- Employee labor and public trust were exploited to serve an equity strategy benefiting a narrow executive circle

ALE Result: Fails all three tests. Reporting was incoherent, inequitable, and designed to conceal rather than inform.

Marketing Integrity Test (MIT)

$$M(C) = \frac{\text{Value Delivered}}{\text{Value Communicated}}$$

$$= \frac{\sim \$100K \ in \ diagnostic \ utility}{\$9.6B \ valuation \ promise \ across \ public \ channels} \approx 0.00001$$

Test: Was value delivered in proportion to what was communicated?

Theranos marketed a diagnostic technology that did not exist in its promised form. Its miniLab machine was showcased in public demonstrations that used pre-tested samples from traditional analyzers. Advertising emphasized rapid results, minimal blood draws, and broad testing coverage — none of which were operational realities.

- Fails **Gate 1 (Figma Fallacy)**: Marketed a functioning device before it was built

- Fails **Gate 2 (Behavioral Manipulation)**: Invoked fear-based marketing, including appeals to military readiness and humanitarian access

- Fails **Gate 3 (Asymmetric Knowledge)**: Withheld critical data about test inaccuracy and failed lab audits

MIT Score: Below 0.50 with all ethical gates triggered. Marketing was not just misleading — it was structurally manipulative.

Market Integrity Equation (MIE)

$$\text{MIE} = \frac{V_{\text{Real}}}{V_{\text{Traded}}} = \frac{\$100,000}{\$9,600,000,000} \approx 0.00001$$

Test: Did the firm's valuation reflect actual contribution?

At peak, Theranos was valued at $9.6 billion. But the company had no commercial technology, negligible revenue, and no FDA-cleared product pipeline.

- Fails **SPG (Speculative Primacy)**: Valuation based entirely on promise

- Fails **LDG (Liquidity Distortion)**: Restricted information and insider control of equity

- Fails **AAG (Access Asymmetry)**: Early investors exited before scrutiny, while employees and late-stage stakeholders bore the reputational and financial fallout

MIE Result: Functionally zero. The firm was priced almost entirely on belief — without a foundation in delivery.

Fair Market Evaluation Test (FMET)

Test: Is the firm under-recognized for its ethical value or contribution?

Not applicable. FMET is designed to protect firms that contribute value but lack narrative momentum. Theranos was over-recognized based on fiction, not overlooked based on substance.

FMET Result: Not triggered. This is a case of hyper-valuation, not undervaluation.

System-Level Conclusion

Theranos was not just a failed startup. It was a breakdown across every level of market logic:

- It extracted public credibility without reinvestment

- It bypassed financial logic through selective disclosure

- It sold a product through narrative, not production

- It inflated value through belief, not delivery

- It misled all stakeholders without consequence until collapse

If the frameworks presented in this book had been applied early in the company's life cycle — by analysts, regulators, or investors — the gaps would have been clear. Theranos would have failed faster, with less damage.

And more importantly, trust in the system may not have been eroded along with it.

Case Study: Costco

The Structure of Quiet Integrity

Costco rarely makes headlines. It doesn't chase innovation hype, dominate earnings calls, or deploy influencer marketing campaigns. And yet, it's one of the most successful and trusted businesses in the world. With a membership-based model, a strong labor reputation, and consistent delivery of consumer value, Costco demonstrates that ethical business practices can scale — even when the market overlooks them.

Viewed through the lens of the five frameworks, Costco does more than pass technical tests — it shows what structural coherence looks like in practice.

Corporate Welfare Equation (CWE)

Test: Does the company deliver more to the public than it extracts?

Costco pays wages significantly above the retail average, offers benefits to part-time workers, and avoids outsourcing critical labor. It invests in supply chain resilience, long-term vendor relationships, and community job creation. There is little evidence of regulatory arbitrage, subsidy abuse, or taxpayer reliance.

$$\text{CWE}_{Costco} = \frac{\text{Public Benefit} - \text{Public Burden}}{\text{Public Burden}} \approx \frac{High - Low}{Low} \gg 1$$

Result: Pass. Costco provides net positive public value.

ALE Analysis: Costco (Fiscal Year 2023)

Costco's 10-K provides sufficient data to apply the ALE Standard using structured reasoning, not subjective interpretation. Here is how the Accountable, Logical, Equitable framework translates into testable criteria using actual data and disclosures.

1. Accountable

Does the firm clearly show who benefits and who bears the cost?

$$\text{Accountability}_{Costco} =$$

$$\frac{\text{Disclosed Stakeholder Cost} + \text{Public Impact}}{\text{Undisclosed/Deferred Liabilities}} \approx$$

$$\frac{\text{Employee Compensation} + \text{ESG Commitments}}{0}$$

- Employee wages and benefits disclosed as part of SG&A: 10.5% of net sales (~$24.7B of $242.3B)

- No evidence of deferred environmental liabilities, hidden tax strategies, or wage shifting to public systems

- Transparent ESG disclosures and long-term supplier contracts

Result: Pass
Costco discloses material obligations, including labor costs, and makes few structural demands on the public. The firm is operationally accountable.

2. Logical

Does the financial narrative follow cause and effect?

$$\text{Logic}_{Costco} =$$

$$\frac{\text{Revenue Model Consistency} + \text{Clear Cost Attribution}}{\text{Financial Contradictions or Narrative Inflation}} = \frac{Strong}{None}$$

- Revenue from operations + memberships is clearly segmented and consistently growing

- Inventory, CapEx, SG&A, and COGS all follow a consistent scale and margin trend

- No speculative valuation inputs, no creative earnings categories, no off-balance sheet ambiguity

Result: Pass

Statements are internally consistent and reflective of the firm's business model. Growth aligns with operational scale, not narrative spin.

3. Equitable

Is value distributed fairly relative to contribution and exposure?

$$\text{Equity}_{Costco} = \frac{\text{Value Delivered to Workers + Consumers + Investors}}{\text{Value Captured by Executives Alone}} \approx \frac{\text{Shared}}{\text{Balanced}}$$

- Workers receive above-market wages, health benefits, and promotional opportunities

- Consumers benefit from reliable pricing and low margins

- Shareholders receive modest but consistent dividends and buybacks

- Executive compensation is high but not extreme by S&P 500 standards, and no golden parachute abuse

Result: Pass

Costco distributes value across stakeholders. No group is over- or under-privileged by design.

Marketing Integrity Test (MIT)

Costco doesn't advertise in traditional ways. Its "marketing" consists mostly of in-store value, limited-time items, and a commitment to low margins.

$$M(C)_{Costco} = \frac{\text{Value Delivered}}{\text{Value Communicated}} \approx 1.0$$

Ethical Gates:

- **Figma Fallacy:** ✖ No forward-promised product launches

- **Behavioral Manipulation:** ✖ No aggressive fear-based or FOMO marketing

- **Asymmetric Knowledge:** ✖ Pricing, sourcing, and policies are transparent

Result: MIT score ~1.0 with no ethical gates triggered. Marketing is minimal, grounded, and aligned with delivery.

Market Integrity Equation (MIE)

Despite its strong fundamentals, Costco's valuation has often lagged behind high-growth tech or retail competitors that deliver less consistency and lower social return.

$$MIE_{Costco} = \frac{\text{Real Output}}{\text{Market Valuation}} \approx 1.2$$

In many quarters, its real contribution (wages, goods delivered, economic stability) exceeds the recognition it receives in speculative valuation.

Ethical Gates:
None triggered.

Result: Passes MIE. May even be underappreciated relative to its systemic value.

Fair Market Evaluation Test (FMET)

Costco is a textbook case for FMET. It:

- Prioritizes fair wages and internal equity

- Minimizes harm to supply chains and communities

- Consistently reinvests in operations, not speculative ventures

- Avoids performance theater while delivering broad utility

$$\text{FMET}_{Costco} = \text{Trigger Activated}$$

Result: FMET justifies its valuation as under-recognized. A rare example of scaled, ethical capitalism.

System-Level Conclusion

Costco succeeds not by gaming the system — but by resisting it. It avoids the short-term thinking that dominates public markets, forgoes manipulative marketing, and consistently builds value through delivery, not narrative. And yet, because of how markets are structured, it often needs a corrective lens — **FMET** — to even be seen clearly.

This is what ethical infrastructure looks like.
Not just passing tests — but making them unnecessary.

Framework as Infrastructure: A Scaffold for Accountability

The frameworks in this book were not designed to replace financial analysis — they were designed to complete it. Each one identifies a different form of distortion that traditional tools overlook. When applied individually, they can help reveal problems. But when used together, they become something larger: a logic system that restores accountability as infrastructure.

This matters because the breakdowns we've covered aren't just symptoms of market volatility. They are the result of a deeper issue: the absence of principled structure in how we test truth in business.

In most companies, performance is measured in isolated dimensions: profit, growth, share price, sentiment. But those metrics fail to ask whether what is being built is viable, fair, or real.

This framework ecosystem solves that problem — not with ideology, but with logic.

- CWE restores accountability to the public.

- ALE ensures that financial statements align with reality.

- MIT tests whether marketing honors consent and coherence.

- MIE challenges valuation to reflect real contribution.

- FMET protects firms that act ethically but go unnoticed by speculative markets.

Together, they offer a new way to understand performance — not as a set of disconnected results, but as a structured evaluation of impact, integrity, and logic.

They also create the foundation for something markets often pretend they already have: a standard.

Not a compliance checklist.
Not a branding gimmick.
A real system — a scaffold — built to measure not just whether a business succeeds, but whether it deserves to.

10   From Logic to Law

Markets rely on structure. That structure does not need to be rigid or prescriptive, but it must be consistent. Without it, decisions are made through instinct, perception, or pressure rather than reasoning. When that happens at scale, systems lose the ability to evaluate themselves, and public trust begins to erode.

Most of the frameworks that guide modern business were not designed to evaluate coherence. They focus on compliance, on operational efficiency, or on risk in narrow terms. While these serve a purpose, they often fail to capture whether a company's operations, communications, and public impact align in a way that is logical, fair, and transparent.

The tools presented throughout this book are designed to support that kind of evaluation. They do not replace financial statements or legal obligations. Instead, they offer structure for interpreting them. They help clarify what is being rewarded, who is carrying the cost, and whether the information available is sufficient to make informed decisions.

In practical terms, these tools can support better governance — both within companies and across institutions. They are not policy instruments on their own, but they can be used to inform standards, shape disclosures, and encourage consistency in how value is measured and communicated.

For example, a municipality considering a public-private partnership could use the Corporate Welfare Equation to determine whether the proposed arrangement would provide a net benefit to the public. A procurement team evaluating vendors could use ALE to assess whether a firm's internal reporting aligns with its operational claims. A review board could use MIT to flag whether marketing communications are overstating capabilities, or leveraging asymmetries in access to information.

None of this requires new forms of enforcement. It requires clearer benchmarks for coherence. The goal is not to increase oversight for its own sake, but to increase understanding. When reasoning is formalized, trust becomes easier to establish and maintain — not through belief, but through process.

It is also possible to apply these ideas in investing and corporate reporting. Institutional investors can use MIE as a screen to assess whether a company's valuation reflects its actual contribution to economic or social outcomes. Where misalignment is found, the analysis does not need to cast blame. It simply adds context to price.

For companies that operate ethically but receive little attention, FMET can serve as a stabilizer. It does not assign a premium; it offers a rationale for recognizing value that markets might overlook. This is especially useful in impact investing or public procurement environments where long-term value and trust are central concerns.

In each of these cases, the same principle applies: logic does not need to compete with ambition. It can support it. These frameworks are not barriers to progress — they are guides for testing whether that progress is meaningful, sustainable, and grounded in reality.

Governance is most effective when it provides clarity, not when it imposes new burdens. The aim is to reduce ambiguity, not creativity. The frameworks outlined here are adaptable. They can be applied informally by internal ethics teams or formally as part of an external audit process. They can support due diligence, improve transparency, or serve as internal checkpoints.

They are not a substitute for law, policy, or fiduciary obligation. But they offer a way to examine whether those tools are being used as intended — and whether the outcomes they produce align with the purpose they were built to serve.

In this sense, structure is not an end in itself. It is a means of holding decisions accountable to logic and fairness. If the goal is to improve the function of markets, institutions, and public systems, then that improvement must begin with clarity. These tools are one path toward achieving it.

11   The Ethics of Choice

Most people don't think of themselves as participants in a system. They think of themselves as individuals making choices within one. That distinction seems small, but it shapes how people interpret their role in economic life. When something goes wrong at scale — when a market collapses, when prices shift unpredictably, when a company makes headlines for misconduct — it's easy to assume those outcomes are out of reach, driven by people and decisions far removed from daily life.

But systems are built from choices. And while no single consumer, employee, or investor defines a system on their own, the structure of those roles shapes the incentives that drive outcomes. That structure becomes more visible when we learn how to test it.

The frameworks introduced in this book were not designed only for regulators or analysts. They were created to offer clarity wherever decisions are made — at any scale. They work in policy, in finance, in ethics committees, and in daily life. They do not require formulas to function. They require attention.

Whether someone is choosing where to work, where to shop, what story to believe, or how to spend time and money, the underlying question is the same: **Does this make sense?** Not just emotionally. Structurally. Can this story be trusted? Can this value be traced? Is this transaction fair?

Most of the time, people are left to answer those questions on instinct. But instinct alone is not enough —

not when systems become more complex, and the costs of distortion become more difficult to see.

These frameworks offer another option: structure as reasoning. They are not tools for judgment. They are tools for alignment. They give us ways to ask better questions, recognize when something is off, and walk away when a decision doesn't feel coherent.

This chapter is about that kind of reasoning. It doesn't offer a checklist. It offers a lens.

The goal is not perfection. It's discernment.

Recognizing Coherence in What You Buy

Most people don't think of a purchase as a structural decision. They think of it as a price check. A matter of preference. Something quick and transactional. And most of the time, that's true. But when certain purchases become habits — when they're repeated, shared, and scaled across millions of consumers — those choices begin to shape the market itself.

This is especially true in a system where branding and storytelling are often more visible than the product itself. Many companies don't compete on price or function. They compete on perception. They win not by delivering better goods, but by appearing more aligned with a lifestyle, a cause, or a trend.

That's where structure begins to matter.

Marketing often tells a story of impact. A product is sustainable, local, revolutionary, equitable. But very little of that can be tested by reading the package or scrolling through a homepage. Most consumers are left to rely on trust — or fatigue. Over time, even the best intentions get buried beneath convenience.

The tools presented in this book offer a way to stay curious, without needing to become cynical. When you consider a company's claims through the lens of MIT, you can begin to ask whether what's promised matches what's delivered. Not perfectly, and not with a formula in hand — but with sharper questions.

- Does the product do what it says?

- Are the terms clear, or hedged in vague language?

- Is urgency being used to pressure a decision?

- Are side effects, tradeoffs, or known limitations being omitted?

These are not philosophical questions. They are structural ones.

The same logic applies to how a company treats its workers. If prices are unusually low, but the business model requires physical labor or constant service, it's worth asking where those savings come from. ALE helps frame that question: Are labor costs transparent? Do outcomes match the operational story being told?

None of this means every consumer choice must be perfect. But coherence is often visible when you know where to look. And once that pattern becomes familiar, it's easier to tell the difference between value that's real and value that's simulated.

This is not about being suspicious of everything. It's about having a way to make decisions that reflect what matters — without needing perfect information, and without treating every claim as equal.

The goal is not to consume less. It's to consume with structure.

Understanding the Companies You Work For

Most people learn more about a company in their first two weeks as an employee than they ever could as a customer. Policies, expectations, priorities — these aren't always written down, but they are lived. Over time, the internal logic of the organization reveals itself. Some companies are consistent. Others aren't.

When that logic feels misaligned, it's often hard to explain why. A company might be profitable, but disorganized. Respected publicly, but deeply inefficient internally. It might talk about values, but rarely act on them. Employees may sense that something is off but struggle to name what's causing the dissonance.

This is where structure becomes helpful. The ALE framework offers a way to evaluate whether a company's internal narrative matches its external one — not through rumor or frustration, but through observable patterns.

If a company seems to be doing well financially, but teams are constantly burned out, under-resourced, or replaced, the equity pillar can offer insight. Who is capturing the benefit of that success, and who is absorbing the cost?

If revenue and recognition are high, but priorities change constantly or deliverables don't seem to matter, the logic pillar may be failing. Are resources being used in a way that makes sense? Is the path between effort and outcome consistent?

If public statements highlight community support or ethical sourcing, but the reality inside the company feels disconnected from those values, the accountability pillar may be weak. Is there transparency in how decisions are made? Are external claims grounded in internal practices?

These aren't issues of culture alone. They are questions of structure. And for employees, being able to recognize that structure can make all the difference — not just in staying or leaving a job, but in understanding why certain problems repeat and why certain solutions never take hold.

No company is perfect, and not every misstep is unethical. But when internal experience diverges too far from external narrative, it becomes difficult to trust the system you're part of. ALE doesn't provide all the answers. But it gives you a framework for asking questions that are often left unspoken — and a way to begin identifying patterns that are not just frustrating, but structural.

Navigating Investment, Advocacy, and Personal Alignment

Not everyone manages a portfolio. Not everyone donates money, leads initiatives, or allocates large budgets. But almost everyone participates in systems that direct capital, attention, or influence. Whether it's deciding where to invest retirement savings, which companies to support publicly, or what causes to endorse, these decisions carry weight — even if they don't feel like it in the moment.

Traditional investment strategies tend to focus on return. Advocacy tends to focus on values. What's often missing is a way to measure whether those things align — whether the company or cause being supported is structured in a way that reflects the outcomes it claims to pursue.

The Market Integrity Equation can be useful here. When considering where to place trust (financial, reputational, or otherwise) it helps to ask whether the organization's market value is supported by real contribution. Is the company being priced for what it does, or for what people hope it might become?

The MIE ratio doesn't require an exact formula to be useful. It begins with a simple observation: Is there a match between how the organization is treated and what it produces? If that gap feels wide, it may be worth pausing before committing further resources.

At the same time, many firms and organizations operate in a way that's steady, consistent, and deeply ethical — but they receive little recognition. These are often overlooked in both investment and media attention. The Fair Market Evaluation Test is designed to help surface those entities — not by declaring them morally superior, but by identifying where market mechanics have failed to reward sustained value.

Sometimes the most responsible companies are the least exciting. They don't chase hype. They don't scale recklessly. They simply do the work. And because of that, they can be easy to miss unless we have tools to detect their contribution.

These frameworks offer more than critique. They offer an alternative way to recognize value — one that supports long-term thinking, shared benefit, and structural coherence.

For those who want to invest or advocate ethically, this kind of clarity is useful. It doesn't demand ideological alignment. It asks a simpler question: *Does the structure support the outcome?*

When the answer is yes, that's often the most durable kind of alignment there is.

Structure as a Daily Practice

Structure doesn't require institutions. It can begin with one person. Most of the frameworks in this book were built from patterns that were visible long before they were formalized — patterns of inconsistency, of overstatement, of value that didn't match effort or output. What made those patterns clear wasn't a credential. It was a process of thinking.

That process can be practiced. It starts by noticing where something doesn't add up, and following that instinct without rushing to judgment. It involves asking whether the pieces of a narrative hold together — not just emotionally, but logically.

This doesn't mean approaching the world with suspicion. It means approaching it with clarity.

And like anything else, clarity becomes easier with the right tools. That's why reasoning should be treated as a skill — not as a talent some people have and others don't. It's something that can be learned, tested, and improved.

The frameworks introduced here are one way to begin that process. But they're not the only way.

For readers who want to keep developing that skill, one of the most accessible and useful texts is *An Illustrated Book of Bad Arguments* by Ali Almossawi. It offers a plain-language introduction to logical reasoning and common fallacies, making it easier to spot when a claim lacks structure — even if it sounds convincing. The book is short, approachable, and focused on application. It's especially useful for those who've never formally studied logic but want to build a foundation they can rely on.

There are many books on critical thinking, but few that make it as clear and usable in everyday life. This one pairs well with the work you've just finished — not because it repeats it, but because it reinforces the habits that give these frameworks strength.

Structure becomes a daily practice when we let clarity replace confusion. Not all at once. Not in every decision. But enough to know when something feels coherent — and when it doesn't.

And once you start to see it, it becomes harder to ignore.

12   The Gate That Never Opens

Market Failure and the Loss of Human Potential

There's a kind of silence that surrounds potential when it's never recognized. Not the silence of rest, but the kind that accumulates around things left undone, ideas left unexplored, and talents left uninvited.

That silence exists in every market. It's the result of incentives that favor confidence over depth, speed over reflection, and visibility over contribution. It's also the product of systems that rarely ask what they're missing.

For every celebrated founder, there are thousands of brilliant people told they aren't qualified. For every inflated valuation, there's a dismissed idea that would've worked if it hadn't needed to scale before it was ready. For every industry built on noise, there are voices that stay quiet — not because they have nothing to say, but because they know they'll be overlooked if they don't speak the language of hype.

This isn't about wasted productivity. It's about wasted clarity.

What gets lost in a system that rewards spectacle is not just truth — but the people who are drawn to truth. People who build quietly, think slowly, work with care. People who could contribute more if the system was designed to recognize what they're already doing.

Instead, many of them end up performing just enough to stay in the game, or opting out entirely. They take jobs they don't believe in, or chase validation through systems they know are broken, because that's the only way to be seen. And over time, they start to question whether their instincts were wrong — whether integrity was ever really an asset to begin with.

That's what this chapter is about. Not burnout. Not disillusionment. But the systemic failure to recognize intellectual human capital when it doesn't look like momentum. And what it might take to change that.

Misallocated Brilliance: How Markets Gatekeep Intelligence

Markets reward what they know how to see. They optimize for signals that are easy to measure — credentials, titles, scale, press, and momentum. And when intelligence doesn't present itself in those forms, it's often ignored, or worse, treated as a threat.

This doesn't happen because markets are hostile to intelligence. It happens because they're indifferent to the kind that doesn't announce itself. Quiet brilliance, unpolished originality, deep internal rigor — these traits are hard to package. They don't create buzz. They don't fit neatly into a resume, a pitch deck, or a LinkedIn summary. And so they get passed over.

For many people, the realization comes early. A job interview that favors confidence over clarity. A project that rewards consensus instead of innovation. An application that filters out talent because it doesn't meet arbitrary benchmarks. Over time, the message becomes clear: the system isn't built to recognize certain kinds of value unless they've already been validated elsewhere.

This is how misallocation happens — not as an exception, but as a pattern. People who could design better systems end up maintaining broken ones. People who think critically about risk are left out of conversations about leadership. People who see through performance are asked to participate in it to be considered credible.

And while the system continues to function, it loses something each time this happens. It loses perspective. It loses resilience. It loses the opportunity to be shaped by people who aren't there to win the game, but to question whether it's worth playing.

These aren't rare individuals. They're common. What's rare is a structure that makes room for them.

The frameworks in this book weren't created just to improve accuracy. They were created to make space — to reward contributions that don't always show up in headline metrics, but that hold systems together behind the scenes.

What's been misallocated can't always be recovered. But it can be recognized. And when it is, the system doesn't just get more efficient. It becomes more human.

Reframing Human Capital as Infrastructure

When people talk about human capital, they usually mean skills, degrees, or productivity. It's treated like an input — something that can be optimized, measured, or monetized. But that definition leaves out the part that matters most.

The real strength of human capital isn't how fast someone can complete a task or how many hours they can bill. It's how they think. How they make sense of complexity. How they approach uncertainty, contradiction, or unfamiliar problems without defaulting to what's already been done.

In most systems, that kind of thinking is invisible unless it comes with the right formatting. And because of that, the market tends to treat it as optional. As a bonus, not a foundation.

But intellectual human capital is not a bonus. It's infrastructure.

It's what keeps organizations from making the same mistakes twice. It's what makes it possible to adapt without chaos. It's what ensures that feedback becomes improvement instead of friction. And yet, in many workplaces and institutions, it remains under-leveraged — valued rhetorically but deprioritized in practice.

This isn't just an issue of management. It's structural. When the systems that assign value are focused on scale, attention, and momentum, slower forms of contribution are often treated as inefficient or unscalable. But in reality, they're the only things that make resilience possible.

When companies fail, it's often not because no one saw the risk. It's because the people who did weren't given the structure to act on what they knew.

Reframing intellectual capital as infrastructure means rethinking what systems are built to prioritize. It means recognizing that insight is not just a personal trait — it's a structural asset. And like any other form of infrastructure, it needs support, reinforcement, and the freedom to do what it's designed to do: create stability through clarity.

The frameworks presented in this book are one way to begin that shift. They don't just test outcomes. They elevate reasoning. They make thinking visible — not as performance, but as a core part of how systems work, change, and endure.

What It Means to Be Seen

Recognition is often framed as reward. A job title, a funding round, a media feature, a promotion. But before any of that, recognition begins with structure. It begins with systems that are built to notice the kinds of contributions that don't always come packaged for attention.

What's most often missing in these systems isn't admiration — it's acknowledgment. The space to be understood without having to perform. The ability to contribute without having to brand the contribution. The permission to think slowly, question openly, and build things that aren't optimized for scale but for coherence.

This kind of recognition isn't passive. It has to be designed. It has to be structured. Otherwise, it gets crowded out — by noise, by momentum, by performance.

That's what these frameworks are ultimately designed to address. Not just fraud. Not just distortion. But the deeper failure of markets and institutions to recognize where real value comes from — and who's producing it, even when no one is watching.

Systems won't change because people want them to. They'll change because the tools exist to support better decisions. And when those tools are used (quietly, consistently, without theatrics) what's been overlooked starts to become visible.

Not because it's louder.

But because the structure now knows how to see it.

Thank You, and Farewell

If you made it this far, thank you.

You're the kind of person this was written for — someone who doesn't need to be told what to think, only given the tools to think more clearly. Someone who senses that something is off in how we measure value, reward behavior, and tell stories in business — and who doesn't stop at that feeling, but wants to do something with it.

This book wasn't written out of frustration. It was written out of resolve.

For a long time, I felt the weight of seeing patterns others ignored. I knew things weren't adding up, but I didn't always have the structure to explain why. That changed when I began applying logic and philosophical reasoning to the business world — not just to criticize it, but to rebuild what might be possible if coherence and integrity were given space to lead.

This is my first book. I don't know how many people will read it. But if it reaches even a few who choose to think more clearly, challenge more gently, or build more deliberately, then that is enough.

I wrote this because I finally feel empowered to share what I've built. The frameworks in these pages are not just tools for analysis. They are invitations. To see with more structure. To engage with more integrity. To help reshape systems not through force, but through clarity.

If we're lucky, this work will contribute to something bigger than itself — a new generation of critical thinkers, and perhaps a set of ethical standards that bring depth and honesty back to how we assess business, risk, value, and trust.

But even if nothing changes overnight, there is one thing worth remembering:

Nothing is ever finished. Not in thought. Not in systems. Not in ourselves.

The work of reasoning — of questioning, refining, and building — is never complete. And that is what gives it power. Because philosophical inquiry doesn't require perfect answers. It only requires that we keep asking better questions.

If this book gave you even one new question worth carrying with you, then it did what I came here to do.

Thank you for reading.

Keep thinking.

www.ingramcontent.com/pod-product-compliance
Lightning Source LLC
Chambersburg PA
CBHW020417150626
46554CB00014B/1901